It's Time to Complete Community College

It's Time to Complete Community College

Student Outcome Studies Show What It Takes to Succeed

S. deBoef

AMERICAN
ASSOCIATION OF
COMMUNITY
COLLEGES

ROWMAN & LITTLEFIELD
Lanham • Boulder • New York • London

Published by Rowman & Littlefield
A wholly owned subsidiary of The Rowman & Littlefield Publishing Group, Inc.
4501 Forbes Boulevard, Suite 200, Lanham, Maryland 20706
www.rowman.com

Unit A, Whitacre Mews, 26-34 Stannary Street, London SE11 4AB

Copyright © 2018 by S. deBoef

British Library Cataloguing in Publication Information Available

Library of Congress Cataloging-in-Publication Data Available

ISBN 9781475840520 (hardback : alk. paper) | ISBN 9781475840537 (pbk. : alk. paper) |
ISBN 9781475840544 (electronic)

∞™ The paper used in this publication meets the minimum requirements of American National Standard for Information Sciences—Permanence of Paper for Printed Library Materials, ANSI/NISO Z39.48-1992.

Printed in the United States of America

Contents

Appendices

Foreword

Community colleges have long been defined by their commitment to being open access institutions. They afford every person, no matter his or her background, an opportunity to advance toward the American Dream. This is absolutely a point of pride for every advocate of the nation's two-year colleges.

It's not enough to be open access, though. During the past decade, it has become abundantly clear that the modern workforce requires more than a high school diploma. Well-paying, in-demand jobs require at least some postsecondary education. And so a shift has occurred in America's community colleges. Leaders have become laser-focused on increasing student success in order to meet the needs of the 21st-century student and the 21st-century economy. Seeing that the United States, once a world leader in college degree completion, was producing fewer college-educated citizens, a challenge was issued to increase college completion rates by 50 percent by 2020.

To help colleges rise to this challenge, the American Association of Community Colleges (AACC) formed the 21st-Century Commission on the Future of Community Colleges. Commission members spent a year listening to higher education stakeholders from across the country, examining long-held practices and policies, and investigating promising practices. In 2012, the commission issued *Reclaiming the American Dream*, a seminal work that provides community college leaders with recommendations to redesign students' education experiences, reinvent institutional roles, and reset the system.

Implementing these recommendations, though, is a tricky thing. Change does not happen overnight, and it will not happen—or be successful—without the support of all members of the college community, particularly the faculty who are typically the people tasked with carrying out new initiatives. S. deBoef understands this. As a faculty member at a community college in Michigan, she is on the front lines every day. She witnesses firsthand the struggles and successes of her students.

In *It's Time to Complete Community College*, deBoef makes the case that student success should not necessarily be measured in retention and completion numbers. Instead, student learning should be the ultimate measure of success. And how can that occur? DeBoef examines influences on student outcomes, such as work, family, and financial pressures.

She includes several ways in which student learning—and therefore student success—can occur. Early interventions, which can happen while the student is still in high school, can help keep students on the pathway to college and career. Support services such as tutoring and counseling also are key to keeping students on the right path. And flexible class scheduling including hybrid and online options are meeting the needs of today's busy students.

One of the recommendations in *Reclaiming the American Dream* is regarding accountability. Community colleges must be accountable to all stakeholders, and in particular, students. To do this, there must be practices in place to measure student learning and growth. DeBoef lays out ways in which faculty can ensure they are truly reaching students and making an impact.

As we barrel toward 2020, community colleges—and higher education institutions in general—have much work to do to reach our goal on completion rates. This cannot be done simply by increasing enrollment numbers. It has to happen by engaging students and supporting them. I commend S. deBoef for her thorough research and for taking an in-depth look at how community college faculty can implement effective instructional methods that can lead to helping both students and institutions meet their goals.

Walter G. Bumphus, Ph.D.
President and CEO, American Association of Community Colleges

Preface

American taxpayers subsidize public colleges because health and well-being are affiliated with college graduation. Approximately half of all college students attend two-year colleges. Twenty-three percent of these students graduate within three years (American Association of Community Colleges [AACC], 2015). The U.S. Census (2015) reports 7 percent of Americans have an associate's degree and 17.4 percent have a bachelor's degree. If educational attainment in the United States were raised to the four-year graduation rates of our Canadian neighbors, real wages would significantly increase (Hanushek & Rivkin, 2010).

It is critical to disseminate and implement institutional and instructional methods that increase student learning and expand rates of educational attainment. Chapters 1–4 of this book summarize theory and research on college student learning. Chapters 5–10 describe research conducted at a public, midsize, Midwestern two-year college articulating instructional practices that support educational goals of students, colleges, and communities.

This book is intended for:

- Students and their families to understand what students can do to learn, and what they must demand from teachers and schools to reach their educational goals;
- Teachers to use to improve instruction, thus learning outcomes of students and institutions;
- Educational administrators and school boards to promote effective teaching and augment student learning and college completion outcomes.

Acknowledgments

The author thanks the college administration and board of trustees (2000–2016) for:

- Permission to access institutional records to conduct research on student learning;
- Financial support to present the research at educational conferences;
- Approval of a semester-long sabbatical to compile the research into this book.

Thus, proceeds from this research are pledged to the college's student emergency fund.

I

COMMUNITY COLLEGE COMPLETION: CONCERN OR CRISIS?

1

The Value of Two-Year Colleges

The word "school" originated with the Latin phrase "leisure for learning" because only those who were not required to labor for survival could participate in formal schooling. The early educational institutions in the United States were reserved for white Anglo-Saxon Protestant (WASP) male property owners, eligible to vote.

As voting privileges expanded, Americans invented public schools because in our participatory democracy, all adult citizens need the capacity to seek evidence to evaluate contradictory claims, understand ballot measures, and elect candidates. "Even more than what you think, how you think matters because we are . . . battling for what it means to be citizens" (Gawande, 2016).

Our Census Bureau (2016) reports that 41.5 percent of U.S. citizens (age 25 and above) have no college experience. This academic breach is critical because education in the United States has traditionally led to economic opportunity. As employers demanded a trained workforce, publicly supported community colleges were created and expanded.

Publicly funded community colleges hold the promise that one can earn a certificate or a degree that can lead to a higher standard of living and fulfilling work. A realistic hope of improving one's life coupled with economic opportunity is associated with lower rates of poverty, crime, incarceration, addiction, mental and physical illness, and other social problems (Quinterno & Orozco, 2012).

The open-door admission policies of community colleges encourage students to enroll regardless of income level, sex, skin color, religion, or previous academic background. Half of all college students in the United States attend two-year colleges. Community college missions pledge student completion of their comprehensive programs. Eighty percent of incoming two-year college students report their intention to transfer to a university (O'Banion, 2016).

Table 1.1. Six-Year Completion and Attrition Rates of Two-Year Colleges*

	Complete/Graduate					
Two-Year Schools	Original School	+	Other Schools	=	Total	Attrition
Full-time	43%		11%		54%	39.5%
Part-time	16.5%		9.5%		26%	70%
All students	26%		13%		39%	43%

*Numbers will not equal 100% due to some students still enrolled and the rounding of percentages. (Trends in Community College Enrollment and Completion Data, Juszkiewicz, 2016).

Yet most two-year students attend part-time, and these students are not represented in the college completion data that reports "first-time, full-time" students. Although completion rates vary between institutions, fewer than 20 percent of two-year college students graduate or transfer within three years (National Center for Educational Statistics [NCES], 2015a). Table 1.1 presents the number of students earning an associate's degree over a six-year period.

Public colleges are asked to demonstrate that student learning is measurable, attainable, and being attained and measured. Completion rates are one measurement of student learning in higher education. Regional accrediting boards assume colleges can be managed as a business. Educators criticize this corporate comparison as misleading because unlike consumers of other goods and services, students share responsibility for producing their learning. Learning involves numerous instructional and institutional factors, inclusive of the students.

TWO-YEAR COLLEGE STUDENT CHARACTERISTICS

Characteristics linked with student persistence include earning college-level math credits, summer session credits, and continuous enrollment with less than 20 percent course withdrawal or repeated courses (Adelman, 2004). Correlates of attrition include having dropped out of high school and completing a General Education Development (GED™) test rather than graduating from high school.

The delay of college entry after high school by one or more years is also associated with failing to complete college. Additional risk factors associated with college noncompletion are part-time enrollment, employment (part- or full-time), being financially independent, and having children (especially single parenthood). A majority of community college students have one or more characteristics associated with attrition (NCES, 2015b; Pruett & Absher, 2015).

High school teachers introduce and instruct learning objectives in class, five days each week. High school typically begins before 9 a.m. and continues at least through 3 p.m. High school students are assigned reading and other homework outside of the school day, to review and practice the information covered in class (Berliner & Glass, 2014).

Unlike high school, traditional college courses meet three to four hours per week with a greater portion of student learning assigned through independent reading, writing, research, and other projects outside of the college classroom. "College students have to do a lot of learning on their own . . . and this gets them into trouble" (Kihlstrom, 2016).

The National Student Clearinghouse (2016) reports that 85 percent of community college students are academically underprepared, testing into developmental reading, writing, or math courses. Forty percent of full-time, first-time degree-seeking students do not complete the developmental courses that they enroll in. Fewer than 10 percent of students who take developmental courses complete their programs of study on time.

Part-time students are a majority of those enrolled in community colleges and test into developmental reading, writing, and mathematics courses in higher numbers than full-time students (Gabriel, 2008). Developmental courses are intended to prepare students for enrollment in college credit–bearing coursework. Colleges that enroll underprepared students without adequate provision of developmental instruction and academic support services provide academic opportunities for failure (Bailey, Jaggard, & Scott-Clayton, 2013).

Underprepared students may not have independent learning skills and they may be unaware that they do not know how to learn on their own. College students need to develop independent study practices to have the same success they experienced in high school. Two-year college students typically underestimate the amount of specific content and time required to learn outside of their classes. College students may skip reading assignments and rely upon a review of (sometimes illegible) notes shortly before an examination (Bjork, Dunlosky, & Kornell, 2013). These tactics may be adequate to complete high school, but they lead to attrition in college classes.

MEASURING INSTRUCTION AND STUDENT OUTCOMES

Despite evidence that student characteristics such as socioeconomic status (SES) and academic background determine academic achievement, community colleges have more control over instructors and instructional practices than over the socioeconomic and other characteristics of their students. "What students do during college counts more in terms of desired outcomes than who they are or even where they go" (National Survey of Student Engagement (NSSE), 2003, p. 1). A large body of research supports that what students do correlates with instructional practice and can be quantified by various methods and sources of data (Banta, 2004; Barefoot & Gardner, 2005).

Institutional factors such as the community's demographics, beauty of the campus, teacher qualifications and pedagogy (what the teacher does to teach), quality of the library, and other resources were once the measure of college success. Educational accountability has shifted from an emphasis on institutional reputation to producing and measuring student learning, a transformation from institutional inputs to a focus on outputs. Today, colleges must have evidence of what a student does to learn and what a student has learned (Morris, 2004, p. 85).

Two-year institutions must monitor student transfer and four-year completion rates to ensure that their courses align with transfer schools (Ellis, 2013). Students who find that they need an additional semester (or year) at a university to complete required courses for their major are overrepresented in the noncompletion data. These students have four years of financial assistance to draw upon and they sustain serious harm when they are directed to complete courses at their two-year college that will not count for the courses they need for their bachelor's degree.

Students are not served when they are allowed to enroll in courses without being informed (based upon their test scores and institutional course completion data) that if they do not devote additional time and resources to supplemental instruction, they are likely to have to enroll multiple times (using up financial aid/loans) to earn the credit. The educational goals of too many community college students are forfeited when supplemental instruction (SI) is not provided with courses that have high attrition rates.

LEARNING IN COLLEGE

Learning is a change in thinking or behavior based upon experience. Experiences that alter thinking or behavior do not have to be firsthand. While learning can be a subjective concept, academicians compare preinstruction knowledge with postinstruction knowledge, measured by some form of testing of the learning objectives. We need about ten thousand hours of practice to become proficient at anything (Gladwell, 2011).

Having the ability to learn is necessary to adapt and survive in any culture. Today, we choose to soak up hours of digital entertainment rather than reading, reflecting, studying, or practicing the skills required for learning. Many habitually obtain instant answers through technology and rarely invest time to develop the skills to search for, understand, and contextualize the meaning of the instant answers provided (Smith & Caruso, 2010; Street, Inthorn, & Scott, 2013).

The advent of the printing press is associated with the growth of democracy, inculcating reading and the sharing of ideas across the social spectrum. Selected soundbites of recorded information simplify news and may even be misleading. Our predilection for keeping our minds busy with superficial entertainment is counterproductive for gaining the ability to become skilled learners.

Teachers are one group of individuals who generally seek out academic challenges and invest in the practice of learning. Teachers devote hours to studying their areas of interest and reading for pleasure. When teachers need to learn new information, they have a broad base of knowledge to build upon, gained over time. Often, teachers have developed the capacity to retain new information by linking it with what they already understand (Corner & Gaffney, 2016).

Teachers dedicate time to reflect on what they are learning and to make active connections, so they can apply the information in their own lives. A conundrum for educators is that students are often unlike teachers in terms of their devotion to the practice of learning. Learning is a skill that does not just happen because we want it to occur. Learning academic content demands the equivalent attention, practice, and guidance required to play an instrument, or to develop a specific athletic skill.

When students do not learn, teachers may excuse their lack of effectiveness by telling themselves that as long as they present the content they are fulfilling their contractual obligations. If someone does not want to learn, no one can make them learn. Yet a teacher can communicate how the objectives are relevant in students' daily lives, ensuring that more students will put forth the necessary effort to learn the content. Although some students do not have the academic background/time necessary for 100 percent success in learning course content, all students can make progress from their starting point.

When we believe that information will be useful and offer advantages, we are willing to do the work necessary to learn. The more a student perceives they are learning, the more they value their education, put forth effort to learn, and the more likely they are to stay and graduate (Tinto, 2000). When students complain that a topic is boring or unimportant, they reveal an ignorance of how the information can be used to benefit their daily experiences (Braxton, Hirschy, & McClendon, 2004). A lack of understanding of how content can be cultivated and employed may be a shortcoming of the instructor, not always of the students.

It is a teacher's responsibility to communicate enthusiasm and the usefulness of their course content. To raise completion rates, the teacher must explicitly model how to study and how to learn the content. When teachers capture a student's interest and have a schedule of assignments that detail what to do and how to do it, more students are successful at gaining expertise beyond what they entered the course knowing and being able to do. A course design with clear descriptions of content and rubrics detailing what competencies need to be acquired, a specific plan for independent practice, and how the content acquisition will be measured results in improved student learning (Blaich, Wise, Pascarella, & Roksa, 2016; Hulleman & Barron, 2016).

Teachers need to provide instruction on learning strategies, design incremental academic challenges, and give students frequent and accurate feedback on their progress. Measurement of student learning is as important for instructors to monitor and improve their teaching as it is for students to monitor their progress to adjust study time and strategies as needed to reach their goals. Many study strategies inculcated by a teacher in one course can be adapted to learn the content of other courses.

College learning requires students to vigilantly employ effective study strategies. Students need to be self-directed to sustain these efforts over time. This explains why some students are successful at learning course content, even with a mediocre instructor. Achievement-oriented students know that they are less likely to learn with an inferior teacher and exit the course sooner, rather than later (Nasser & McIrney, 2016).

Less experienced students stay in the course, not knowing what they need to do to learn, hoping that learning will occur if they diligently attend class, read the assigned textbook, and use a highlighter. When independent learning is necessary, with or without a proficient instructor, there are likely to be higher rates of student attrition and failure (Tinto, 2016). These findings imply that student ability does not always correlate with student course performance or learning.

HIGHER EDUCATION RESEARCH ON STUDENT OUTCOMES

Educational psychologists call for empirical studies on student learning at the course level because when multiple groups are combined, meaningful information can be lost (Bonesronning, 2004). A study of 257 community college classrooms across 32 community colleges in 11 states that reported "good" versus "distressed" instruction found "unacceptably low" student, course, and program completion rates (Grubb, 1999, p. 350). Based upon these conclusions, teachers were advised to develop instructional strategies to support student completion. Some educators resist the exploration of instructional effectiveness in terms of student outcomes and dispute the need to investigate student learning or attrition at the course level.

The American Educational Research Association (2011) developed ethical standards for teachers to measure learning and to link educational goals with outcomes (AERA, pp. 145–156). These principles include:

- Require attention to outcomes and to the experiences that lead to those outcomes;
- Determine how to meet the needs of particular students;
- Emphasize deep, rather than surface learning;
- Adhere to a standards- and evidence-based outcomes approach to instruction.

Analyzing instructional practices and student outcomes is essential because "teaching does not occur in the absence of learning" (Bain, 2004, p. 173). A meta-analysis of factors that influence learning found that when teachers evaluated their impact upon student learning and used the results to modify their practice, instruction was correlated (93 percent) with academic success (Hattie, 2011).

Research conducted by teachers using their classroom data is most often undertaken for institutional assessment in higher education. Assessment is guided by specific questions: "What are we doing in terms of goals and objectives? Is what we are doing working? What and how well are students learning? How can we know using our data gathering techniques and assessment tools? What changes or adaptations do we need to make?" (Rouseff-Baker & Holm, 2004, pp. 30–41).

Educational literature indicates that measurement of student learning requires the review of a number of sections of the same course for each instructor, rather than averaging outcomes for combinations of courses and instructors across disciplines. Assessment of student learning following this protocol can identify specific modifications for enhancing student learning outcomes (NSSE, 2015).

College administrators may require faculty to submit course and program assessment reports for accreditation purposes "to check off compliance." Sometimes these reports are not reviewed, nor are the recommendations applied to improve course- or program-level student learning outcomes. Assessment research rarely has an audience beyond administrators, accreditors, and educational conference participants (Haertel, 2013; National Research Council, 2008, 2015).

Many call for practitioner research to reach a broader audience so that findings can be replicated to expand the body of knowledge regarding the measurement of, and support for, student learning (Wieman, 2017). Yet teacher research is customarily engulfed in a rising tide of institutional data, occasionally published on a college or conference website. Due to these conventions, teacher/practitioner research has been called "renegade research," indicating that the information exists outside of traditional forums of professional peer-reviewed journals and books.

The knowledge and credentials acquired in higher education have incalculable value. Encouraging college access without providing students instructional and institutional supports to accomplish their academic goals results in student debt without degrees. Considering expenditures for public education combined with distressing rates of two-year college attrition, it is vital to determine policies and procedures that achieve the promise of community colleges.

2

Measuring Student Learning

Higher education accreditation standards mandate that *faculty* manage and monitor student learning using appropriate procedures and maintain legal and ethical expectations, including student retention. Administrators and faculty are required to analyze data about teaching practices and student learning, to augment student performance. Teachers often make changes from one semester to another based on student outcomes related to course content and instructional techniques (Fink, 2013).

The reasons for the instructional changes are seldom documented beyond different assignments or adjusted scoring rubrics across an instructor's subsequent syllabi. Assessment is a method to document instructional practices associated with student learning outcomes. Using assessment data to measure and improve educational practices is phrased as "closing the loop" or "bridging the gap" between research and practice. Figure 2.1 portrays an assessment model adapted from Butler and McMunn's (2006) *Classroom Assessment Cycle* (p. 214) and Halpern's (1993) *Iterative Outcomes Assessment* (p. 44).

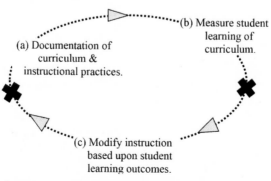

Figure 2.1. Broken Assessment Cycle

Figure 2.1 portrays student outcomes as a measure of instruction. This diagram reveals that assessment findings are seldom used to measure or inform instruction. The broken model shows a one-directional process unlike the proscribed iterative cycle designed so that results of the measures collected are used to improve instruction and student outcomes.

Assessment as practiced at many institutions does not:

A. "Document curriculum and instructional practices"; provide evidence that the best instructional practices for a specific curriculum and group of students are employed
B. "Measure student learning of curriculum objectives"; are curriculum objectives aligned across course sections and comparable with university transfer courses? How do we know that student learning objectives (SLOs) are multidimensional, valid, and reliable?
C. "Modify instruction based upon student outcomes"; how should instruction be modified for a specific curriculum or group of students to enhance learning outcomes, as demographics, culture, and technology continue to change?</ll>

The primary goal is for the results of assessment to be applied to improve teaching, learning, and delivery of services to students. Some colleges require assessment follow-up reports that oblige faculty to identify instructional strategies implemented and to document whether the strategies improved student learning (Banta, Jones, & Black, 2009, p. 21). Student enrollment and retention goals must be secondary to student learning because "institutions that are serious about what students learn make the most significant strides toward ensuring student success" (Upcraft et al., 2005, p. 6).

Higher education accrediting agencies underscore assessment's number one priority: using the results to develop programs and services for students, emphasizing that "assessment is a vehicle for improvement, not an end in itself" (Banta, Black, Kahn, & Jackson, 2004, p. 10). Assessment to establish benchmarks may reveal best practices and how these practices can be applied to create a learning organization.

BENCHMARKING

Benchmarking is the creation and use of a system to determine effectiveness and implement improvements to reach specified standards (Mirriam & Cafferella, 1999, p. 8). In an educational context, benchmarking has occasionally been termed "bench-learning because benchmarking begins with self-assessment at the student and course level to develop baselines, to explore student outcome patterns, and to uncover performance gaps" (Van Middlesworth, 2003, p. 11). Benchmarking obtains comparative numbers on varied outcomes, between students, courses, programs, and schools, to decipher patterns in student outcomes.

To understand outcomes for each student at the course, program, and institutional level, well-defined measures of course competencies must be delineated.

Documenting the extent that these competencies are acquired can "allow institutions to compare changes over time, both at the aggregate and granular levels" (Friedlander & Serban, 2004, p. 103). Granular levels of the student and course section are recommended because the aggregation of outcome measures across course sections, disciplines, and departments can mask actual variation, called "the ecological fallacy."

The measurement of student learning requires the review of a number of sections of the same course for each instructor, rather than averaging outcomes for combinations of courses and instructors across disciplines. Assessment of multiple sections of an instructor can identify specific modifications for enhancing student learning outcomes (Kinzie, Cogswell, & Wheatle, 2015). Benchmarking is one method of accountability for instructors, departments, and institutions (Ohmann, 2000, pp. 1–2).

Researchers recommend data "be disaggregated into meaningful subgroups . . . [to] be valuable for program improvement [because] comparative institutional data are not always available" (Borden & Owens, 2001, p. 12). The difficulty of comparing student outcomes across courses, programs, and institutions due to the lack of universal instructional standards and content is a limitation of benchmarking (Walvoord, 2004).

For example, teaching practices, assignments, methods of assigning grades, and grading scales vary between teachers and can make comparisons of student learning on the basis of student grades problematic (Friedlander & Serban, 2004). Unstandardized measures of student learning across courses, programs, and schools provide

> no reliable way to determine the . . . quality of undergraduate work that lies behind the grade. One would need subject-by-subject samples of student work responding to the same prompts, judged by the same faculty members using the same criteria, over two or three decades in order to determine the relationship between grades and performance. (Adelman, 1999, p. 198)

Instructors need to forge common measures of student performance in order to create parity across a specific course (American Psychological Association, 2015). When comparable course content and grading standards are developed through collaboration between faculty and administrators, stakeholders can assess performance and understand whether students are experiencing similar levels of learning across course sections and instructors.

Benchmarking is a recommended method to monitor the quality of outcomes, make data available, and prompt implementation of best practices. Benchmarks of student outcomes must be balanced with the autonomy and academic freedom granted to faculty in higher education (Theall, 2001).

ACADEMIC FREEDOM

Higher education faculty are granted autonomy because of the role of education in the United States. Faculty need freedom of inquiry, to speak out, and to teach according to the best methods derived from their academic disciplines (Fossey & Wood, 2004). Academic freedom is a pillar of democracy that ensures that an educated public has the ability to access, comprehend, and evaluate information to perform the duties of citizens of our country, and the world (Hamilton, 2002).

Academic freedom "is predicated on academic rigor that backs up thought . . . the expression of ideas with intellectual integrity, the liberty to publish ideas that might go against the grain or take on risky ideas" (Lewis, 2015). Academic freedom does not establish a right to practice anyway one pleases. Professional autonomy obligates teachers to deliver course content responsibly (Darling-Hammond, 2000).

College faculty are expected to uphold high standards and fulfill public service. Faculty are responsible for more than dispensing information; they structure student learning, regularly designing and assessing improvements (Boggs, 2004). Faculty develop methods to measure what students are learning (National Research Council, 2001). Those who teach the same course need to work together to develop learning objectives and grading methods of the specified levels of competencies.

Multiple measures of topic-focused student work should be graded with standardized, criterion-referenced grading protocols (Marzano, 2003). Course standardization is necessary for the comparison of student outcomes across course sections, to establish benchmarks, and set enrollment, performance, and retention goals. Faculty are charged with establishing competencies for each course and routinely measuring and documenting the degree that each student has met the course competencies as a measure of instructional and institutional effectiveness.

The necessity of articulation agreements between educational institutions for the transfer of course credit has resulted in some standardization across courses, programs, and schools. Faculty autonomy can be an impediment to the collaboration required to build curriculum and assessment practices across courses, disciplines, and colleges. Academic freedom does not permit faculty to subvert higher educational goals, such as the accurate measurement of student learning.

Academic freedom allows teachers to use subjective measures of student learning such as effort and attendance. Multiple measures of grading are desirable to gauge the depth of understanding, the ability to apply underlying principles to novel problems, and to afford reliability and validity of student learning measures. Beyond test scores and grades, student surveys of their course experiences are measures of learning and instructional effectiveness across course sections (American Academy of Arts & Sciences, 2016a).

STUDENT EVALUATION OF INSTRUCTION (SEI)

Surveys designed for students to report their learning experiences at the end of a course are called student evaluation of instruction (SEI). Standardized test scores and SEIs are important measures to corroborate grades submitted by teachers. SEIs are sometimes discussed in educational literature as student evaluations of teaching (SET). Records of student enrollment, performance, and attrition, together with student evaluations of instruction indicate student learning at the course level (Johnston & Kristovich, 2000, p. 68).

The National Survey of Student Engagement (NSSE) reports that favorable classroom experiences and instructional best practices are associated with students achieving their learning goals because higher engagement levels, learning, and good grades are correlated (Kuh, Kinzie, Buckley, Bridge, & Hayek, 2011). SEI research concludes that students value learning and rate courses highly when they learn, independent of their grade earned in the course (Boretz, 2004; Marsh & Roche, 2000).

There have been more than two thousand studies validating SEI (Boysen, 2016). SEI is used by educational researchers as an outcome measure of instruction because student ratings of their learning in a course correlate with external measures, such as student achievement test scores, continued enrollment (persistence), and student attrition (Thompson & Serra, 2005). The majority of higher education institutions in the United States use some form of SEI (Marsh, 2007).

Figure 2.2 portrays associations between student descriptions of their learning and their performance outcomes (including persistence and attrition). This diagram, based on research results of Seiler and Seiler (2002), shows that low student test scores and high attrition correlate with students' reporting deficient learning and inferior quality of the course. Students enrolled in poorly rated courses are more likely than those enrolled in highly rated courses to withdraw from the class, sometimes from all classes (Moxley, Dubrigue, & Najor-Durack, 2001).

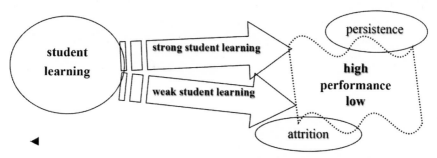

Figure 2.2. Student Evaluation of Instruction Learning Correlations

Some instructors are unconvinced about the validity of student reports of their learning, claiming that positive student evaluations reflect less coursework. These reservations are unsupported, based upon the finding that either "too much" or "too little" coursework results in low student evaluations with 90 percent of students in agreement regarding a given course (Isely & Singh, 2005). The level of student agreement confirms that a few students with personality conflicts or work disputes with an instructor will not be able to sway the evaluation system and undermine the validity of course evaluations (Aultman Price, 2006).

Faculty may worry that students lack maturity or the expertise necessary to judge course content and instruction. SEI research substantiates that students consider the amount they learned and the fairness of tests heavily (Secolsky & Denison, 2011). Much of the SEI research finds that college students use reasonable weighting schemes (Dougherty, Hilberg, & Epaloose, 2002). The difficulty of course content, fairness, and the amount learned "are questions that students are in a position to answer best" (Harrison, Ryan, & Moore, 1996, p. 780).

Students possess substantial self-insight regarding their overall evaluations of instructional effectiveness within and between disciplines (Beran & Violato, 2005). The validity of SEI is corroborated by students' attribution of poor performance to their own lack of effort/ability, as well as specific course characteristics (Davis & Hillman Murrell, 1994). SEI is unaffected by a variety of factors when intervening variables are controlled, including class size, amount of work required, and college level of the students.

For example, when large classes include group work or other methods of student-to-student and student-to-teacher interaction, these courses do not receive lower evaluations than courses with fewer students. When student evaluation criteria are multidimensional, relevant, and reviewed in aggregate, student reports of course workload, challenge, fairness, and the amount of student learning are verified (Dunn, Mehrotra, & Halonen, 2004, p. 233).

The frequent replication of SEI studies (although each study is not identical) is considered a strength of the research (Richardson, 2005). SEI research typically uses large samples, such as Centra's 2003 study of more than fifty thousand courses. Perry (2004) reports that he initiated thirty years of research to refute the validity of SEI surveys, and that his findings have thus far confirmed the validity of aggregate student evaluations of instruction. SEI research conveys that college students prefer challenging, well-taught courses compared with easy or poorly taught courses (Young & Zucker, 2004).

Students rate courses with challenge more favorably than unchallenging courses in a curvilinear relationship as portrayed in figure 2.3. Beyond a certain point, excessive

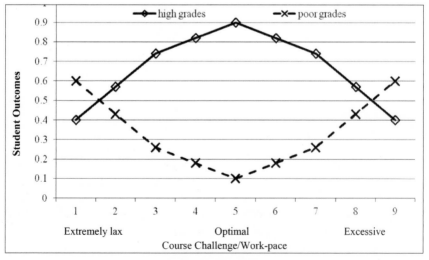

Figure 2.3. Course Challenge and Student Outcomes

work with a pressured pace decreases instructional effectiveness and student learning. Appropriate academic challenge is described as coursework that is not so easy that it is perceived as boring busywork, or so difficult that it appears impossible to achieve.

Courses with either "too little," or "too much" challenge leave students frustrated with their lack of understanding of course content (Harrison, Ryan, & Moore, 1996, p. 780). Course characteristics that correlate with high student ratings include appropriate challenge, fairness, and students' perception that they learned in the course (Heckert, Latier, Ringwald, & Silvey, 2006). Overloaded students report few feelings of success and feel forced to accept less in terms of their learning to manage the quantity of material, while those who are not challenged value the course less and become disengaged (Greenwald & Gillmore, 1997; Marsh & Roche, 2000).

Many college teachers design their courses and instruction according with the content in the textbook they require their students to purchase. College teachers rely on test banks, PowerPoints, notes, diagrams, simulations, and video clips provided by publishers of college textbooks. Publishers strive to include any material that a teacher could conceivably want, so that a range of teachers with different interests within a discipline will choose to use the text. U.S. publishers in America produce textbooks "three times as thick as those in other nations" to gain the broadest market (Bracey, 2006).

The International Association for the Evaluation of Educational Achievement (IEA) reported many more topics covered by American teachers than European or Asian teachers, "resulting in instruction that is shallow and too brief" (Bracey, 2002, p. 135). Textbooks and resources that accompany texts are tools to be used by instructors and students. Too often in the United States, the textbooks and technology resources drive the educational process and undermine student learning.

Bain (2004) characterized "two acid tests" of successful teaching—"students highly satisfied with the teaching" and "students learned"—and insisted that student reports of course instruction are not "a mere popularity contest" (pp. 7–8). SEI research supports a strong relationship between positive instructional performance ratings and student learning and retention (Spooren & Mortelmans, 2006). Appropriate academic challenge results in motivated students who learn and persist (Kember, 2004).

Students enrolled in introductory social science courses often represent the population of two-year students who intend to transfer to a university. Student enrollments in upper-level courses are measures of student learning and emotional experiences in introductory courses and signify continued interest of the student in a discipline (Johnson, 2003). To ensure student learning and integration into the college, introductory courses should be assessed annually, including an administrative review of SEI for all courses.

Students who experience some connection with an instructor are more likely to learn and to persist. Educational research affirms that learning reflects a dynamic interaction between student, instructional, and institutional factors. However, little consensus exists among researchers regarding how, or to what degree, each of these elements influences student learning and student outcomes (Clark & Smouse, 2017; Kiziliak, Safarelli, Reich, & Cohen, 2017).

3

Academic Inputs and Student Learning Outcomes

The Scholastic Achievement Test (SAT) and the American College Test (ACT) are the standardized college admission tests that determine course placement within many colleges. Hundreds of studies have concluded that student college admission test scores correlate with college grade point averages (Astin & Oseguera, 2002).

When college admission test scores declined in the 1980s, worldwide publications predicted that the United States was slipping in competitiveness (National Research Council, 2001). Averaging the college admission test scores of a broad range of students across socioeconomic statuses (including low SES, associated with substandard academic opportunities) predictably reduces the average of student scores.

In earlier decades in the United States (and currently in many other countries) elite students were selected to take these tests (Bracey, 2006, p. 18). Today, most high school graduates are encouraged to complete college entrance tests and participate in some form of higher education in the United States (Romainville, 2002). American taxpayers provide extensive financial support for public education because public colleges are intended to benefit all citizens. Student tuition represents a fraction of a college budget (College Board, 2014).

Some portion of tuition originates with state and federal funds allocated for student grants and loans. Admission test scores at two-year colleges with open-door policies are used to determine course placement and need for additional institutional resources. Inclusive admission policies amplify the need for programs and expenditures that will help students to achieve academic and career goals.

Colleges that admit students that are not academically prepared are obligated to provide scheduling and student services that support the success of these students. Students might need to take fewer courses when they have limited familiarity in a discipline, to allow more time to accomplish course objectives. Students are not often able to receive financial aid when enrolled part-time, and there has not been an increase in the time frame of a college semester.

> Colleges may say they care about their students, but caring isn't the same as understanding their needs and designing [resources to meet] them. Colleges that place students at the center of their decision-making will have the best chance to close the gap between what students need and what they are getting (Culatta & Speicher, 2016, p. B25).

UNDERPREPARED STUDENTS

National admission test scores indicate that half of students entering two-year colleges have less than a 10th-grade level of reading, writing, or math skills. These scores prompt enrollment in prerequisite courses to prepare students for college-level courses. These prerequisite courses are called developmental/remedial courses. Developmental courses have less than 50 percent pass rates, and fewer than 20 percent of these students go on to complete college-level courses. Students who are directed to enroll in developmental courses may exhaust their financial aid prior to earning their two- or four-year degree (O'Shea, 2017).

Perhaps a better use of public education funds would be for all 10th-grade students to be tested. Those identified as needing developmental courses could dedicate their junior and senior years of high school to raising their reading, writing, and math skills to be prepared to satisfactorily complete college-level courses upon high school graduation.

High-achieving students are encouraged to enroll in college courses while still in high school. Early college programs are intended to raise rates of college graduation. Students in these programs are often the same motivated students who would complete a college degree after high school. Given that fewer than a quarter of U.S. citizens have a four-year college degree, creating a developmental pathway for high school students who are not academic high achievers while they are still attending high school is warranted.

Student enrollment and attrition are opposing sides of a student's goal. A student's exit from an institution prior to completion is "attrition," whether the goal is one course, an earned certificate, or an associate's degree. Enrollment in upper-level courses is progress toward reaching the student's goal. Although individual student withdrawal can be a result of health, family, employment, or transportation challenges, the rate of student-related reasons for exit tends to be fairly low and consistent across courses (Hartlep & Forsyth, 2000).

HIGH-RISK COURSES

The equivalency of student grade point averages between those who complete and those who withdraw indicates that attrition is infrequently due to a lack of student ability or effort (Tschannen-Moran & Hoy, 1998, p. 14). Thus, rates of student attrition can be utilized to identify problematic or promising courses and programs in higher education (Leathwood, 2005, p. 312).

Rates of student course withdrawal can be compared to acceptable benchmarks of a specific course to be used as a measure of student learning. When students drop, they are essentially firing the teacher and forfeiting time, money, and effort expended. High rates of student withdrawal (compared with similar courses with lower rates) expose "low quality or demeaning instruction [where] students . . . vote with their feet" (Grubb, 1999, p. 59). Withdrawal reflects a student's course experience, not student capability, because students must have test scores documenting their reading, writing, and math skills to enroll in a college-level course.

Courses with 30 percent (and higher) failure and withdrawal rates are considered "high risk." To raise student completion rates, two-year colleges must identify high-risk courses and provide training for the instructors, support for students, and revise course scheduling. Identifying students who are struggling and providing interventions based upon the individual student need can improve student persistence (Nilson, 2013; Kezar, 2014).

Institutional support can consist of tutoring or supplemental instruction designed for courses identified as "high risk." Unfortunately, some educators view their work as sifting and sorting, rather than developing students' academic proficiency. This educational philosophy is called the gatekeeper approach/academic Darwinism (Young & Zucker, 2004, p. 129). The utilization of institutional records such as enrollment and attrition to determine areas for improvement has been haphazard given the gatekeeper approach of some administrators and faculty.

Gatekeepers consider attrition to be a student problem, "nature's way of separating the wheat from the chaff" (Upcraft et al., 2005, p. 5). These faculty and administrators are hesitant to implement practices that contribute to students' success. The gatekeeper approach is contradicted by the majority of college students that have the ability to be successful, though some may need additional preparation/support services.

A FORMULA FOR ACADEMIC LEARNING

The Cooperative Institutional Research Program (CIRP) Freshman Survey (2004) concluded that 77 percent of freshmen nationwide "attend college to learn more" (p. 8). If this sentiment is accurate, two-year college attrition rates demonstrate that half of these students are disappointed in their learning. Student learning is a complex, ill-structured construct that is difficult to measure because student learning outcomes tend to defy a single explanation and require multitheoretical approaches.

Student learning can be conceptualized as a product of student, instruction, and institutional characteristics (Dunn et al., 2004, p. 232). In 1977, Astin developed the Input-Environment-Outcome (I-E-O) model to guide student outcome studies. This model discusses student outcomes as a function of the inputs (background and abilities of entering students) and the environment (everything the student experiences in college).

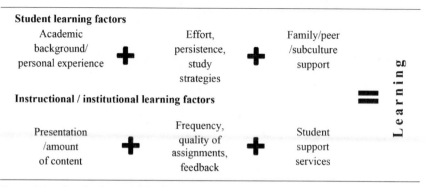

Figure 3.1. Academic Learning Theory

Student characteristics can be supported or undermined by instructional and institutional components. Factors that play a role in the sum of learning can be identified. Figure 3.1 summarizes major factors that impact student learning and educational outcomes, organized as a Formula for Academic Learning.

Student characteristics. Academic background and self-discipline in terms of effort put forth and persistence, along with study strategies practiced by a student, are part of what determines student learning. However, zip code is the strongest predictor of college achievement, because one's address is correlated with socioeconomic status (SES) (Benjamin, 2015). The proportion of children reared in poverty has surged in the United States over the last thirty years, with concurrent increases in the number of students completing ACT/SAT (United Nations Children's Emergency Fund (UNICEF), 2005).

Research on SES generally confers a strong positive correlation with test scores. Per college entrance test scores and federal financial-aid statistics, more students are enrolling in two-year colleges with lower reading, writing, and math skills, and qualifying for financial aid, than in previous generations, (AACC, 2016). While the level of parental income is one of the strongest determinants of academic success, parental education is another.

First-generation students are those whose parents did not attend college. These students typically have lower SAT/ACT college entrance test scores (Atherton, 2014). The percentage of ACT-tested graduates who are first-generation students has almost doubled from 10 to 18 percent (Abdul-Alim, 2015). Students in two-year colleges are primarily from lower-, working-, and middle-class socioeconomic backgrounds, living with their parents/their own children.

In 1960, the average American citizen spent one-third of their income on food. The Social Security Administration multiplied the cost of the least expensive diet (identified by the Department of Agriculture) by three to determine the threshold of poverty in the United States. This system continues to be used, despite the average food plan to-day costing one-fifth of a family's income while housing, childcare, medical treatment, and transportation costs each consume a larger proportion of a family budget. Housing in the twenty-first century is estimated to deplete half of a family budget.

According to the U.S. Census Bureau, 13.5 percent of Americans live in poverty and 33 percent live close to poverty (DeNavas-Walt & Proctor, 2014). If poverty was measured more accurately, such as using the cost of housing as the base rate, Americans counted as living under the threshold of poverty would be much higher.

The effects of poverty on educational progress are more debilitating than any other demographic status. Economically disadvantaged students have higher rates of requiring remediation. Again and again, researchers confirm that low SES correlates with less satisfactory educational outcomes due to disadvantages associated with poverty (Schudde & Goldrick-Rab, 2017). Table 3.1 presents two-year student characteristics.

Table 3.1. National Two-Year College Student Demographics

Full-time student employed	Full-time	22%	} 62%
	Part-time	40%	
Part-time student employed	Full-time	41%	} 73%
	Part-time	32%	
Dependent children	With partner	23%	} 40%
	Single parent	17%	
Age	21 and younger	37%	
	22 to 39	49%	
	40 plus	14%	
Race	African American	14%	
	European American	50%	
	Hispanic American	21%	
	Other racial status	15%	
Sex	Females	54–57%	
	Males	43–46%	

American Association of Community Colleges (AACC), 2017.

Table 3.1 reveals that a majority of two-year students work and attend school part-time due to work, family, and financial constraints. At least 70 percent of college students work 30 or more hours weekly (Fang, 2013). College students who are employed 15 hours or more each week frequently earn lower grades and have lower completion rates (Perna, 2010). More economically disadvantaged students are enrolled in college today than in previous decades, and these students require more institutional supports to complete their educational goals.

The diversity of students requires the expansion of educational practices, services, and scheduling to allow them to meet their academic goals in conjunction with their family, employment, and military commitments. In addition to SES and employment status, research links sex of the student to their outcomes. Sex of students, as noted in table 3.1, varies by 3 percent across sources from year to year. More than half of all college students today are women, and they persist at higher rates than men (Juszkiewicz, 2016).

Analyses of student characteristics are relevant to identify patterns for interventions that support student success. For example, a national study revealed that age at time of initial entry into college makes a difference in students' outcomes. When students are below age 24 at enrollment, they have a 36 percent likelihood of persisting to the second year (NSC, 2016).

Those 24 and older are often financially independent from their parents/have dependent children. The rate of persisting to the second year of college drops significantly for older students. Current students compared with those of earlier generations

- Are less academically prepared;
- Are more culturally diverse;
- Are more often nontraditionally aged;
- Spend more time working in jobs unrelated to their career aspirations;
- Are more likely to have children;
- Are more likely to originate from economically disadvantaged backgrounds.

The composition of students in higher education today, in terms of socioeconomic status, educational preparedness, age, and other status continues to expand. Due to the diversity of current students, colleges need to adapt to meet these students' needs for affiliation and identity (Abdul-Alim, 2015). Contemporary students perceive themselves as having little in common with their classmates, on and off campus. LGBT students, international students, religious minority groups, students of color, those of nontraditional age, in or veterans of the military, and students with disabilities report a perception of institutionalized incivility.

If a student belongs to a peer group/family/subculture that does not value education or does not support the student's decision to study and participate in educational activities, it is less likely that the student will be successful (Chetty, Friedman, Saez, Turner, & Yagan, 2017). Those that do not value education will pressure the student with alternatives (such as social activities or family obligations) that interfere with educational goals. When students perceive employment opportunities, they may opt out of education, to earn income. Research suggests that some income today has more value for students from a lower SES background than the possibility of higher income in the future.

According to the "Expectancy X Value" calculation of motivation, academic success obliges a student to value education, and based upon previous experiences, expect that they have the ability to learn in college (Wentzel & Wigfield, 2009; Shechter, Durik, Miyamoto, & Harackiewicz, 2011). Valued alternative opportunities undermine the motivation to achieve academic goals.

College characteristics. Student characteristics interact with institutional factors like campus climate and curriculum. Due to a slow pace of curricula transformation to reflect pluralistic beliefs, customs, values, and worldviews, campus climate can be perceived as resistant to multiculturalism. A campus climate that does not value diversity negatively impacts student performance. The importance of inclusive classrooms and campus services to support the educational achievement of all students must be emphasized (Bambara, Harbour, Davies, Gray, & Athey, 2009).

Open-door community college policies allow students (many without the academic background or family or peer support of previous generations) to enroll. These students become absorbed into colleges and classrooms that may not provide needed support services. Institutional investment in student support services such as open computer labs, library resources, tutoring, and testing centers (where students can make up missed tests) amplify two-year college completion rates (Demin & Dynarski, 2010).

Two-year college resources must remain available across weekdays, through weeknights, and weekends. The failure to identify students who need academic supports and require these students to draw upon needed academic services has been labeled "providing the opportunity to fail." Encouraging students to enroll in college with financial aid, without provision of instruction and support services needed for student success, detracts from potential economic mobility and harms individuals, families, and communities (Looney, 2017).

College tuition has significantly increased in the past twenty years due to diminishing federal and state support. A majority of two-year college students work and are enrolled part-time. Their part-time student status limits their financial aid and benefit options, including access to health care (Orozco & Cauthen, 2009). National student data report that 62 percent of those who drop out of college are responsible for paying for their own education. Another 30 percent of students who received financial assistance and withdrew from college remain responsible for repaying student loans (Quinterno & Orozco, 2012).

Attending college detracts from economic security until achieving degree status. College graduates earn an average of 17,500 dollars more, annually, than high school graduates (Kurtzleben, 2014). Although two-year college student educational needs have been documented through various indicators, initiatives implemented to meet these needs have been fragmented and underfunded.

National two-year college attrition rates above 50 percent after 3 years illustrate that many colleges are not providing the student services and scheduling essential for these students. Thus, it is critical to identify and implement strategies that support students enrolled in two-year colleges to achieve their educational goals.

4

Instructional and Institutional Practices and Student Outcomes

Student outcomes are an important source of evidence of instructional effectiveness because learning is viewed as a product of the interaction of students with instructional characteristics. Instructional factors include both instructor and course characteristics because instructor personality and capability coincide with instructional methods chosen and implemented by an instructor.

Higher-education accreditation standards generally require instructors to have earned a minimum of a master's degree in the subject they teach, or a master's degree in a related discipline with 18 graduate credits in the subject that they teach (Higher Learning Commission, 2016, p. 1). A master's degree typically consists of 60 graduate credits including thesis research in a specific content area. A master's degree takes 2 or more years beyond the bachelor's degree (minimum of 120 credits, typically earned in 4 or more years).

Early childhood education through 12th-grade education majors are required to complete educational psychology courses that communicate how to apply the research on human development, cognitive science, learning, motivation, and assessment in classroom teaching. Bachelor's and master's degrees without an education major are unlikely to include coursework or assignments on recommended teaching practices, or to require supervised student teaching (Kezar & Maxey, 2014).

INSTRUCTIONAL PRACTICES

Instructional practices that result in high rates of efficient and effective student learning are often identified through replicated research in educational settings. These methods are called "best practices" or "high-impact" instructional practices. College teachers who become skillful, quantified by high rates of student learning, take it upon themselves to study and employ best practices. Expert teachers construct a framework to guide students to identify the relevant information of a problem set, showing novices where to focus attention and expanding the amount of information (cognitive load) that can be attended to and recalled (Valcke, 2002).

Instructional characteristics are consistently found to correlate with student persistence (Habley, Bloom, & Robbins, 2012). Instructor content knowledge, pedagogical expertise, fairness, enthusiasm, and respect for students are positive correlates of student learning. Instructors who believe that students have the ability to succeed (efficacy beliefs) provide the instruction needed to galvanize student effort, and these students make academic progress (Browers & Tomic, 2001).

Motivating student interest increases their effort. When students become interested in a course, they put forth more effort in the course, learn more in the course, and enroll in another course in the discipline at higher rates than those students whose interest is not piqued, regardless of course requirements in their chosen field. "The more students learn . . . the more likely they are to persist, and when . . . student success, satisfaction, and learning [coincide], persistence is the outcome" (Noel-Levitz, 2012, p. 1).

Research confirms that the highest-achieving college students do well independent of course instruction. Achievement-oriented students seek methods to learn course objectives outside of class when necessary, to maintain their high levels of performance (Winne & Nesbit, 2010). Achievement-oriented students know that they are less likely to learn with an inferior teacher.

When motivated students cannot find strategies to maintain high performance in poorly taught courses, they typically withdraw from the course, sooner rather than later. Less experienced students often stay in a course, not knowing what they need to do to learn, hoping that learning will occur if they diligently attend class, read the assigned textbook, and use a highlighter. When independent learning is necessary, with or without a proficient instructor, there are likely to be higher rates of student attrition and failure (Tinto, 2016).

Often college teachers use the instructional methods that they experienced as college students: lecture with high-stakes midterm and final exams. These practices may be adequate for university students, but completion rates indicate that these instructional practices are insufficient for many students enrolled in two-year colleges. According to Graesser (2011), Canning and Harackiewicz (2015), Taylor and Parsons (2011), and others, pedagogical expertise associated with student learning includes:

- Communicating enthusiasm for course content and building course organization on incremental, clear, and quantifiable objectives;
- Explicitly showing how the content can be gainfully applied beyond the classroom and requesting students to examine connections between their experiences and the content;
- Developing a variety of instructional methods that correspond with specific kinds of objectives, to support differing student strengths;

- Scheduling course workload/pace that is neither excessive nor lax, and allows students to practice and build to higher levels of competence;
- Establishing frequent opportunities for a variety of low-stakes assessments that allow students to perform in at least one area of proficiency;
- Advising students to expect obstacles and setbacks. Encouraging students to work through difficulties, while demonstrating that learning demands effortful practice over time;
- Modeling a variety of study strategies such as consistent self-testing, creating mnemonics, and visual aids. Conveying that when a study strategy is not productive, to use a different strategy and seek help from the teacher;
- Providing frequent corrective feedback using standards-based measures of achievement of course objectives, so that students can determine how they are progressing and adapt their strategies to reach their goals (Doherty et al., 2002; Wendorf & Alexander, 2005).

Grading standards and practices implemented by an instructor provide insight into the priorities of an instructor and the relationship between instructor and students. Teacher-to-student and student-to-peer relationships are implied through grading policies designed to provoke competition or to promote cooperative and collaborative learning (Stiggins, 2005). Grading policies can denote whether an instructor's authority or student learning is paramount, and whether evaluation procedures are communicated or concealed (Brookhart, 2004). Public colleges are charged with the responsibility to uphold fair and reasonable grading practices.

INSTITUTIONAL CHARACTERISTICS

The ethos of an institution can support or undermine student initiative. Community college student diversity signals that two-year colleges must provide academic and personal counseling as well as referrals for community social services. Two-year college student services include academic, personal and career counseling, financial aid advising, librarians, and computer consultants. Colleges need to guide students through the complex financial aid process because financial aid is instrumental for many to enroll.

Financial aid. Financial aid is often counted as income by government agencies though the funds go directly to tuition, fees, and books. This policy undermines obtaining needed supports for a student-parent with no, part-, or full-time employment who earns minimum wage. Scholarships, grants, work-study, and other kinds of financial aid were never intended to provide housing, utilities, childcare, food, medical, or transportation needs of students/their children (American Association of Arts & Sciences [AAAS], 2016).

How does a parent choose between accepting financial aid for tuition to improve the family's economic circumstances and losing housing, food, energy, childcare, or other assistance programs for their family? Financial aid is distributed for tuition, and a parent must sacrifice work hours that generate income. These are decisions that students are forced to make and that can compel a family to remain in poverty across generations.

Colleges proudly advertise libraries, computer labs, test centers, and other services but may not have these needed resources staffed and open around the clock. Students who work/are parents require access to college services at all hours. If a college cannot keep libraries and computer labs staffed and open twenty-four hours a day, then students may be shut out of the time needed to research, write, and submit college assignments and tests around their parental/work responsibilities.

When states withhold financial investment for higher education, needed programs and services are cut, resulting in an increase in attrition for those students who most need these services. Two-year colleges are more accessible in terms of location and affordability for many low- and middle-income citizens. Citizens must continually petition state legislatures to ensure financial investment for public education (AAAS, 2017).

Administrative oversight. Research demonstrates that teachers can improve their courses if an administrator reviews student evaluations of instruction (SEIs) with the instructor (Weaver, Watts, & Maloney, 2001). Colleges with high rates of student success require SEI in every class and use the aggregate scores for each instructor to identify areas for improvement. Inferior teaching is not acceptable in high-achieving colleges. Institutions with high student completion rates create and utilize an effective process for replacing substandard administrators, faculty, or staff (Lundenburg & Ornstein, 2004).

Although many instructors will voluntarily seek to institute best practices, some instructors may require administrative intervention to proceed. College administrators who utilize teacher performance appraisal systems, including SEI, are in a better position to make decisions and use their budgets to enhance, rather than to derail, students' educational aspirations (Kilgo, Ezell Sheets, & Pascarella, 2015). Performance appraisal requires systematic evaluation of performance, corrective feedback, and motivation for improvement.

A decade of multisection research of instruction comparing SEI with and without feedback from administrators to teachers found that teachers who received feedback subsequently received higher end-of-term ratings in 20 of the 22 comparisons (Cohen, 1988). When feedback included an interview with a pedagogical consultant, course ratings increased from the 50th to the 75th percentile by the end of the semester.

These well-designed studies determined that "correlational effect sizes . . . were remarkably stable under a variety of conditions and methodological manipulations" (Cohen, 1988, p. 78). These findings demonstrate that SEI reviewed by administrators and discussed with instructors can be used productively for diagnostic feedback for improvement of instruction and enhanced student learning. "Faculty evaluation should be [based upon] documented student learning outcomes, because if these are low, the institution is clearly not successful in this mission area" (McPhail & McPhail, 2006, p. 96).

Institutions of higher education (IHEs) are charged with collecting and utilizing institutional data to ensure that instruction is meeting or exceeding standards of their mission statements. Administrators with titles including "of instruction" or "of academics" are advised to review lesson plans, examinations, student work, and classroom records because these course artifacts reflect how well a teacher has thought through instructional goals.

Measures of learning. A review of classroom records such as tests and assignments can indicate how well a teacher has linked instructional goals and testing (McKeachie, 2002). "For teachers to find out whether they've taught well, the extent of student learning must be determined" (Popham, 2005, p. 339). Administrators must measure instructional outcomes and provide training and release time for ongoing teacher training.

Student performance in college is traditionally calculated with course grades. However, the Higher Education Report (2004) contends that disparate standards of grading limit the credibility of grades as a measure of student learning. The reliance upon grades as an indicator of student learning endures due to the absence of other measures. Student persistence, measured by continued enrollment over time in an institution, demonstrates that students are learning. Attrition rates provide a measure of the absence of student learning and are a barometer of the health of an institution (Seidman, 2005, p. 5).

IHEs utilize grading pervasively for evaluation and promotion of students. Thus, understanding how grading practices influence student learning represents an important area of research. There is a need for empirical and longitudinal evidence to confirm the growing body of anecdotal evidence reporting fluctuating standards and disparity in grading practices, philosophies, and policies. Analysis of grading practices and student learning at the course level is needed to unravel the effects of heterogeneous grading policies on student outcomes.

IHEs with robust student performance and completion have administrators, faculty, and staff who work together with a strong sense of purpose and belief in their ability to successfully guide students through academic programs. A learning outcomes approach advances a shift from the institutional priority to provide grades for ranking students, to an emphasis of obtaining student performance outcomes for the evaluation of institutional effectiveness (Burke, 2006).

These concerns are described as assessment *of* learning (assignments to determine grades) versus assessment *for* learning (assignments designed for students to master content). Assessments for learning are typically smaller, graded assignments that include the opportunity for students to correct their work (mastery learning). The shift from the assumption that learning is strictly the student's problem to multiple levels of shared responsibility encourages administrators to be more aware of the connection between faculty support and student success.

Support services. Two-year college administrators must ensure the provision of support staff to contact underperforming students and direct these students to tutoring and other needed services. Institutional support for instructors and students includes the identification of "high-risk" courses, in order to attach supplemental instruction (SI) with these courses. As discussed, a "high-risk" course is a course "with 30 percent or higher rate of 'D's', 'F's', or withdrawals . . . thirty percent of two-year colleges offer SI linked to one or more killer courses" (Upcraft et al., 2005, p. 57).

Open-door colleges must provide counseling, tutoring, test centers, and assistance in libraries and computer labs—services that have been validated for increased student success at two-year schools (Scrivener, Weiss, & Teres, 2009). Two-year colleges need to have a minimum of 75 percent of courses taught by full-time instructors (Eagan & Jaeger, 2009). Full-time instructors at two-year colleges should have maximum annual teaching loads of eight courses consisting of no more than thirty students. Lower enrollment caps are recommended for courses that are writing intensive.

These parameters allow faculty the time necessary to provide detailed feedback to individual students, and time for faculty development (such as ongoing educational technology training). Institutional factors include instructional support (provision of computers, copy centers, etc.) and required professional development (including release time and financial support for conferences/travel to conferences).

"Colleges should provide faculty [full- and part-time] with training and technical support to develop meaningful and measurable student learning outcomes . . . and ensure that assessment of student learning outcomes are used consistently by all faculty members" (Friedlander & Serban, 2004, p. 106). Evidence of learning outcomes consists of exactly what and how much students have learned.

MEASURING STUDENT PROGRESS

Student achievement is associated with "a challenging, engaging, and empowering learning environment that builds upon interests, abilities, and prior learning" (Ratcliff et al., 1996, p. 12). An organizational culture of high expectations, respect for students, and transparency for stakeholders correlates with students' success. According to AAAS (2017) and CCRC (2015), high-achieving colleges, including those that enroll economically disadvantaged students, require:

- High academic standards with a belief in students' capability to fulfill the standards;
- Ongoing faculty training of mastery-oriented instructional techniques that enable students to exercise more control over their academic performances;
- Provision of release time for learning management system (LMS) training for all faculty, so that students can access their assignments, grades, classmates, and teacher outside of class;
- Free available student training of computer and LMS technology, with computer labs and technical assistance available around the clock, seven days a week.

Two-year institutions need to support student clubs, extracurricular speakers, drama, and experiential learning. Students are enriched by their investment in these activities, and those who participate are more likely to complete their educational goals.

Two-year institutions must foster strong relationships with local schools, businesses, taxpayers, and transfer schools to support the transition of students across institutions (Massey, 2016).

Colleges are required to "demonstrate their value" (Freedman, 2016, p. B8). "Measuring graduation rates and early-career earnings, though not without challenges, is much easier than measuring student learning, given the absence of agreed upon measures" (Arum, Roksa, & Cook, 2016, p. 3). Current measures of student learning include grades, certificates, number of college credits earned, degrees in educational settings, and student transfer.

Student transfer from a two-year college to a university is a cumbersome indicator of student progress because of "swirl" patterns of students moving between community colleges and universities in both directions, over time. Yet two-year college attrition and persistence can be measured and can indicate avenues for intervention and budget allocations. To ensure the measurement of student learning, Pallas, Neumann, Campbell (2012) and others, recommend that administrators require:

- Curricular objectives aligned across course sections with multiple indicators of course competencies such as standardized test scores and examples of student work;
- Instructors to use similar criterion-referenced grading practices aligned with specific course competencies (equivalent to the best colleges) to reflect student learning outcomes for transparent, meaningful benchmarking standards;
- SEI submitted by all students in every class (including students who withdraw) because student-reported learning is associated with strong performance and low rates of attrition. SEI reviewed by master teachers with the evaluated instructor, for improvement of subsequent student learning;
- Benchmarking comparisons of student performance and attrition at the teacher, course, and discipline level, to flag promising/problematic courses and programs for the distribution of institutional resources.

High course-level student performance and persistence determined by criterion-referenced (not norm-referenced) grading indicate high instructor expectations and positive engagement with students. These elements can and should be measured, with goals set and monitored across time, for an institution of higher education to truly be a learning organization.

Due to the lack of curricular standardization, few college-, discipline-, and course-level studies on differences in student performance have been conducted. Performance indicators such as course grades and college completion rates are generated annually. Yet these data are not commonly used as comparative course and departmental measures or distributed to academic and student-support departments for self-assessment or planning.

II

HOW DO INSTRUCTIONAL PRACTICES INFLUENCE STUDENT OUTCOMES?

5

A Study of Student Outcomes
in a Gateway Course

Foundational, high-enrollment courses with elevated attrition rates are called "gateway" courses. Students who successfully complete gateway courses in their first year have higher rates of college graduation. First-time, full-time students are tracked in the National Center for Education Statistics, though the majority of two-year college students are not first-time, or full-time, and over half of these students do not complete a two-year degree, or transfer to a university (2015a).

Seventy percent of students enroll in an Introduction to Psychology course (Landrum & Gurung, 2013). Introduction to Psychology is a gateway course that undergraduate students commonly choose within their first year to fulfill a social science requirement for an associate's/bachelor's degree. Students' classroom experiences in the first six months to one year of college impact their rates of retention (Tinto, 2016). Therefore, the experiences of students in Introduction to Psychology courses are prognostic for student retention and college completion.

A faculty researcher requested and was granted permission to access and analyze course data to investigate instructional influences of student outcomes across Introduction to Psychology courses. The public two-year college provided student enrollment records and course syllabi for the introductory psychology courses over a six-year period of fall and winter semesters ($N = 5{,}940$). Large multisection designs are recommended to study the effects of instruction on student outcomes, yet are scarce in educational literature (Arthur, Tubre, Paul, & Edens, 2003, p. 283).

According to educational law, archival data (student demographics, enrollment, grades, and instructor syllabi) do not belong to the students or to the faculty, but to the academic institution (Kaplin & Lee, 2006, pp. 311–312). When administrative consent is given and no identifying data is collected, there is no requirement for instructors or students to grant permission to conduct research using the college data.

The data was collected from the courses of the four full-time instructors. The sample consisted of the first 15 consecutive on-campus courses, scheduled 1 hour each between 9 a. m. and 3 p.m., Monday through Thursday, of each full-time instructor. The part-time instructors did not each have the required number of courses over the time frame to be included in the study. Institutional data consisted of student entrance test scores, sex of the student, final grade, and course syllabi.

Triangulating multiple institutional measures such as student characteristics, course artifacts (documented in syllabi, standardized examination scores, student work, student evaluations), and student grades (A through fail and withdraw) is recommended for comparing student learning across course sections. Examples of student work, student test scores, or evaluations of their courses were not available.

The sample (N = 1,710) was less than the 30 students per section expected (N = 1,800) for peak weekday, fall and winter courses. The sample was further reduced by the removal of 96 students who were enrolled in courses within the sample multiple times. To avoid participant duplication, the 96 students who took the class beyond their first enrollment were removed from their subsequent enrollment/s, yielding a research sample of 1,614 students.

Allowing students in the data multiple times violates the assumption of independent observations necessary to complete statistical analysis. This sample size is adequate for correlational research "conducted so that relationships between variables can be examined, but none of the variables can be considered a treatment or an intervention in the lives of the subjects" (Katzer, Cook, & Crouch, 1991, p. 247).

The outcome variables for the study comprised final grades of students, including W for withdraw. Sometimes student departure is called attrition, withdrawal, or drop rates, and sometimes the phenomena are examined in terms of student attainment of their stated goals, whether this is a certificate, degree, or transfer. Sometimes reenrolling is considered "persistence," and National Student Clearinghouse data indicates "completion" as earning a degree via completing courses from one or more institutions (2016).

This study systematically analyzes student characteristics and instructional practices for student performance (A through C) and attrition (D through F, fail, and W, withdrawal) at the course level. This research constitutes an ex post facto design, to reduce potential for researcher bias, because "the researcher has no control over the predictor variables . . . [that] occurred in the past, before the researcher considered doing the study" (Katzer, Cook, & Crouch, 1991, p. 249).

STUDENT CHARACTERISTICS

Public two-year colleges have more control over instructional practices than over student characteristics, because community colleges are "open-door" institutions. An open-door institution allows student enrollment without requiring evidence of student college readiness, such as high school transcripts, General Education Development (GED™) certification, or college entrance test scores. However, these sources can be mined to determine the appropriate level of course placement for students.

There is ample evidence that student characteristics do influence academic achievement (Frey, 2016). As discussed, student zip code, student college entrance test scores, and parental education and income are predictors of educational achievement. These factors are all a measure of socioeconomic status (SES), including family expectations and financial support for higher education. Higher SES is associated with a lifetime of enriching experiences that support academic success versus the likelihood of falling further behind with each summer break from formal education.

Factors outside of higher education such as a student's physical and social environment, as well as a student's alternative options to college have been implicated as influences of academic outcomes (U.S. Census, 2016). For these reasons, student characteristics that could be documented were included to control for potential influence of student outcomes in the psychology course. Due to the ex post facto design, characteristics not provided for the students in the sample include:

- parental income/level of education,
- amount of hours of student employment,
- full- or part-time college status,
- age of student,
- living with parents or living independently,
- having dependent children.

This information is relevant because students who juggle multiple roles such as student-employee/student-parent/student-athlete have higher demands on their time and lower graduation rates (Perna, 2010). The sample of 1,614 students across 60 courses is large enough to be representative of students enrolled in liberal arts courses in the two-year college. Thus, the characteristics of students enrolled in the college offer a general description of students in the sample.

Student demographics. This study was conducted in a midsize (approximately 5,000 students), two-year college in the Midwest. This college reports that 78 percent of students enrolled are degree seeking. The sample represented 27 percent of students enrolled in the Introduction to Psychology course during the six-year time frame of the study at the institution. During the research period, 4 percent of students were age 18 and below, 43 percent were 19 to 21, 27 percent were 22 through 29, and 26 percent were 30 and above.

Age of students attending this two-year college mirror those enrolled in the national two-year college population for the time period. Eighty percent of students in this two-year college were high school graduates, 15 percent completed a GED™ certificate, and the remaining 5 percent were high school students taking college courses. Students attending this college are primarily from lower-, working-, and middle-class socioeconomic backgrounds, living with their parents/their own children.

An indication of SES reported by the National Census Bureau is median household income of 53,657 dollars for full-time workers in 2014—not statistically different from previous years for an average family household of three to four individuals (DeNavas-Walt & Proctor, 2014, p. 5). Because working-class families have less income than middle-class families, it is likely that many of the students attending this two-year college were from families subsisting below the median household income.

Students who complete 12 to 15 credits in at least one semester of college are statistically more likely to graduate, and to graduate in two years for an associate's and four years for a bachelor's degree (CCSSE, 2017). Full-time students who work less than 20 hours per week also have higher rates of college completion. It is not known if these associations are due to students with higher SES allowing them to be full-time students/to work less.

Regardless, students who work less and enroll full-time most semesters complete more courses in less time, incrementally increasing completion versus falling behind, getting older, and needing to work full-time to be financially independent/support children (NCES, 2015b). Student characteristics available in the registration records at the community college consisted of the sex (male or female) and ability (college entrance test scores) of students.

Student sex and ability. Sex and ability data of students were collected and analyzed to rule out potential impact upon course performance. These characteristics are relevant because previous research concludes that females earn higher grades in social science courses and that college entrance ability scores predict student performance. The sex and ability variables of students were predicted to be similar for students across the course sections and thus to have little if any influence on student outcomes across the four instructional groups.

Most community colleges in the United States use a system for determining if a student is "College Ready'" or needs one or more "Developmental" courses prior to enrolling in college-level courses. Achievement tests "assess how much students have learned from what they have specifically been taught" while aptitude tests "assess students' general capability to learn" (Ormrod, 2006, p. 585).

Both types of tests convey academic ability that predates a student's experience of college instruction. American College Testing (ACT) and Scholastic Aptitude Test (SAT) are promoted for their prediction of a student's college performance, in terms of student grade point average (GPA). Forty-seven percent of students in the sample had college ACT/SAT entrance test scores.

The High School Proficiency (HSP) is a state high school senior examination that can be utilized as an academic competency score for two-year college course placement. Seventy-four percent of students in the sample had HSP examination scores. The HSP test provided three levels of ability that could not be calibrated into the ACT or SAT scores.

The highest HSP score indicated that students were "College Ready," that is, eligible to enroll in college-level courses. The ASSET Planning and Placement Test developed by American College Testing Services consists of reading, writing, and math skill tests that are used to determine student college course placement for those students without ACT, SAT, or HSP reports. Forty-eight percent of students in the sample had ASSET scores.

All of these test scores (as provided in the registrar data) were used to indicate student ability prior to their enrollment in the introductory psychology course. Students who did not have test scores recorded (7.5 percent) were permitted to enroll by a teacher or counselor with academic knowledge of the student. When more than one test score was recorded for a student, the higher score was used to determine course placement. Multiple ability test scores were compatible 90 percent of the time.

The intention was to calibrate ability levels of students in the sample with their SAT/ACT scores. However, the majority of students in the sample did not have an ACT or SAT score listed in the registration data. The registrar data included a High School Profile (HSP) score for 74 percent of students, overlapping with some records of ACT or SAT scores. Table 5.1 lists the student ability and sex information of the sample, the college, and national two-year college data.

Table 5.1.   Student Characteristics for Sample and Population

Characteristic		Sample	Midwestern Community College*	Two-Year College Population**
Ability	College Ready	80.0%	75.4%	50%
	Developmental	12.5%	24.6%	50%
Sex	Females	64.0%	60.0%	54%
	Males	36.0%	40.0%	46%

*Midwestern Community College Impact Statement, 2010; **AACC, 2016.

The Placement Test Codes Plan and Ability Conversion Formula for Student Entrance Test Scores uses ACT/SAT/HSP/ASSET test scores for placement in either "College Ready" (college credit-bearing courses) or one or more "Developmental" courses (remedial course/s recommended to prepare the student to enroll in a college-level course). According to this test-ability score conversion, 80 percent of the students in this sample were "College Ready" and 12. 5 percent completed one or more developmental courses prior to enrolling in the courses of interest.

Sex of the student (male or female) as documented in the institutional record was entered into the analyses to control for its possible influence on student performance because females typically earn higher grades than males in social science courses (Volkwein, 2003). The proportion of females to males reflects contemporary demographics of more females enrolled in college than males in two-year colleges, as well as within the broader population of college students (U.S. National Center for Educational Statistics, 2015). The Placement Test Codes Plan and Ability Conversion Formula used by many two-year colleges is presented in appendix A.

COURSE SYLLABI

Course expectations must be clearly communicated for students to manage their time to meet the demands of their courses. Syllabi serve as the foundation of a college course, documenting reading, writing, testing, and other assignments. Explicit course organization in a syllabus allows students to prioritize assignments and schedule time to do the work.

Course syllabi document elements of course instruction such as type of grading practices, text, chapters, curriculum topics, reading assignments, and the array of opportunities for student assessment such as papers, presentations, tests, and class attendance. Research on instructional practices concludes that grading practices and workload (also referred to as "challenge" or "work-pace") are associated with student learning (Guskey, 2013).

The college syllabus template required the following information (*Mid-sized, Midwestern College Handbook*, 2010):

1. A calendar of student responsibilities, including reading and writing assignments, laboratory reports, due dates, and the schedule of examinations;
2. Methods of assessing student performance, including examinations (comprehensive final examination or otherwise) and writing requirements;
3. Specific grading criteria and the grading scale (including plus and minus grades);
4. Policies regarding make-up of missed examinations, late assignments, failure to turn in an assignment;
5. The attendance policy and the effect of attendance on a student's grade.

Syllabi are used to compare course objectives and content across course sections and institutions to document course comparability for institutional articulation agreements. Accrediting bodies look to syllabi to "ascertain what happens in specific courses and then look across syllabi to gauge learning . . . within a specific discipline" (Habanek, 2005, p. 160). Content analyses of course syllabi provide systematic, indirect measures of course instructional practices. Content analysis techniques are advocated for educational research because these measures are less intrusive and cannot be influenced by the investigator (Elton, 2004, p. 121).

The sample of four groups included two instructional groups (of 15 courses each) with norm-referenced grading and two instructional groups (15 courses each) with criterion-referenced grading. The number of text chapters, pages, and additional sources of reading were tallied and sequenced across the instructional groups, as documented in the course syllabi.

INSTRUCTIONAL GROUPS

Textbook pages of assigned reading were counted because all instructors did not use the same textbook, or assign the same pages when they required the same textbook.

Differences such as illustrations and practice tests that affected the average words per page were taken into account. This information serves as a measure of the instructional variable of course difficulty, pace, and workload (labeled *work-pace*), over the semester as depicted in table 5.2.

Table 5.2.   Description of the Four Instructional Groups (*N* = 1,614)

Instructional Group	Assigned Reading + Extra Credit Opportunities	Grading + Feedback Opportunities	Grading Practices	
			Criterion-Referenced	Norm-Referenced
Criterion, work-pace 1	300 pages (13 text chapters) + extra credit available	10 tests + comprehensive final, 3 (5 pg.) papers	438 students (27%)	
Norm, work-pace 2	463 pages (14 text chapters) including supporting article pages + extra credit available	7 tests, no comprehensive final, no papers		402 students (25%)
Criterion, work-pace 3	492 pages (16 text chapters) no extra credit available	4 tests + comprehensive final, 20 worksheets	389 students (24%)	
Norm, work-pace 4	646 pages (19 text chapters) + additional article pages assigned & not counted, no extra credit available	7 tests + comprehensive final, a research paper, + group presentation		385 students (24%)
Total			827 students (51%)	787 students (49%)

Table 5.2 reports the sequencing of the instructional groups ordered from lowest (1) to highest (4), and represents the *work-pace* measure. Characteristics that undermine learning "include (a) excessive amount of course material, (b) lack of opportunity to pursue the subject in depth, (c) threatening and anxiety-provoking assessment" (Rhem, 1995, reported by Upcraft et al., 2005, p. 248). Moderate course work-pace provides opportunities to understand the connections between new content and life experiences.

Triangulating chapters, number of pages, tests, papers, presentations, and extra credit opportunities added credence that these indicators of course work-pace were reliable measures. The number of tests and papers assigned were included as an indication of feedback opportunities for students. The more feedback students receive on their course progress in the form of graded assignments, the better they are able to adapt and practice study strategies to improve their academic performance.

Although the work of teaching can be reduced with fewer graded assignments, a decrease in opportunities for students to earn points results in each assessment counting for more of the course credit. That is, insufficient graded opportunities comprise high-stakes, high-anxiety assignments/tests for two-year college students likely struggling with work, children, financial, and other constraints.

Type of grading practices (criterion- or norm-referenced) provides context to understand variability of student outcomes across instructional groups, sequenced by work-pace. Rubrics for assignments to support amount and pace of content were not available in the syllabi for all instructional groups and could not be analyzed. Relevant portions of the course syllabi for the instructional groups are provided in appendix B.

6

Course Grading Practices and Work-Pace

Instructional practices described in gateway course syllabi include grading methods and workload, also called work-pace. Classroom grading matters because this traditional measure of student learning drives teacher pedagogy. Grading practices have the motivational capacity to encourage or inhibit learning, along with the function of evaluating learning outcomes. Table 6.1 shows how the levels of grades from college records equate with performance or attrition for the study of instructional practices and student outcomes.

Table 6.1.   Student Grade Outcomes

1) A, A– 2) B+, B, B– 3) C+, C, C–	1) performance
4) D+, D, D–, F (fail), W (withdraw)	2) attrition

To investigate the effects of instructional practices for student outcomes, final grades of D were combined with F (fail) and W (withdraw) because the institutional grading policy stated that students were not allowed to enroll in an upper-level course unless earning a C or higher in their introductory-level course. When a student failed a course, reenrolled, and earned a higher grade, the previous course grade was changed to a W. W could be entered as a final course grade at the discretion of an instructor or submitted by the student prior to the last week of the course. Students receiving financial aid might request an F grade, rather than a W, because a grade of W could disrupt financial aid.

The criterion-referenced, work-pace 1 syllabus (for 15 courses) indicated that the instructor would submit a grade of W one week prior to final examinations for those students who did not have enough points to pass the course, unless the student requested a grade of F, to preserve financial aid. The W grade would be submitted in lieu of a failing grade of F to allow students the option of retaking the course without impairing their grade point average. Relevant portions of the syllabi from the courses studied are presented in appendix B.

A grade point average below 2.0 reflects some proportion of grades below C and delays student transfer, because universities typically require transfer students to have GPAs above 2.0 (C equivalency) for a student to enroll. The norm-referenced, work-pace 2 and the criterion-referenced, work-pace 3 syllabi (for half of the students in the sample) indicated that Fs would be submitted if a student did not attend a certain number of days, whether or not a student was passing or submitted a course withdrawal form.

According to student evaluation of instruction (SEI) research, there is a strong positive relationship between grades received, standardized test scores, attrition, and student evaluations of their learning (Elton, 2004; Darling-Hammond, 2016). The "grade-leniency theory" of SEI correlations suggests that instructors attempt to "buy" high student evaluations with "good grades," while the "instructional-effectiveness" explanation argues that students evaluate instruction in terms of their learning, and that grades accurately reflect student learning.

In the few studies that show no relationship between student evaluations of their learning and their course grade, inscrutable grading practices are considered to have obscured the correlation (Marsh, 2007). For this study, college administrators reported that SEIs were not required by the college for every class. Instructors at the college were required to choose one course annually for evaluation.

When student evaluations were administered, they were not reviewed by the administration or retained by the college. According to this college-wide SEI policy, it is unlikely that the theoretical instructional strategy "to grade leniently in exchange for high student evaluations" was a factor of student performance within this study's sample of sixty courses. In any case, the teacher-researcher was not granted access to student evaluations pertinent to the courses in the study as an additional measure to triangulate the data/corroborate the findings.

GRADING PRACTICES

Grades are positively correlated with gains in general education, practical competence, and personal-social growth (Seybert, 2004). The National Center on Post-Secondary Teaching, Learning, and Assessment reported that "grading is the sole means of assessment and accumulation of credits is the sole indicator of student learning" (Ratcliff et al., 1996, p. 42). Yet learning is ambiguous to measure because it is a process that requires subjective criteria to be made as objective as possible.

When grading disparities exist (as they frequently do), teachers "are running a different currency system than used in the world in which they live" (Walvoord & Johnson Anderson, 1998, p. 102). College institutions influence "curriculum content, choice of curriculum materials, grading policies" because student learning outcomes are a key verification of institutional effectiveness (Fossey & Wood, 2004, p. 60).

Research on grades as the measurement of student learning concludes that grades are problematic because faculty who teach the same course rarely consult with one another to ensure that students receive comparable grades for comparable work (Guskey, 2009). The faculty of the courses studied elected not to collaborate to create standardized course objectives, comparable course content, a final examination, or a pool of questions for a final examination that could be administered across the course sections and instructors.

One study of 12,500 students across several disciplines found that the type of grading practice used significantly affected the distribution of student marks (Hornby, 2003). The primary types of grading methods are criterion-referenced (also called standards-referenced/absolute) and norm-referenced (grading on the curve/relative grading).

Criterion-referenced grading. Criterion-referenced grading compares student performance on a task to a standard or criterion to assess student proficiency (Tan & Prosser, 2004, p. 276). Educational psychologists support criterion-referenced scoring based upon standardized instructional objectives as the most appropriate method for grading decisions (Brookhart, 2004, p. 72).

Assignments should be communicated with rubrics delineating a scoring system of levels of competency that result in specified points. Transparent approaches that undermine arbitrary cut-off points are endorsed to allow students to monitor their progress (Marzano, 2007). Criterion-referenced grading tends to result in divergent patterns of student learning that convey the quality of course instruction and student learning. Criterion-referenced grading provides insight on academic progress that permits students to make adjustments necessary for learning (Robbins, Lauver, Le, Davis, Langley, & Carlstrom, 2004).

A meta-analysis of 21 studies found that using criterion grading with rubrics increased student achievement by 32 percentile points (Fuchs & Fuchs, 1986). Another study that compared criterion- and norm-referenced grading found that the achievement of students in criterion-referenced courses was 14 percentile points higher than for those in norm-referenced courses (Wilburn & Phelps,1983, as cited by Marzano, Pickering, & Pollock, 2001).

Norm-referenced grading. Norm-referenced grading formulas result in a predetermined, evenly distributed pattern of student outcomes. Norm-referenced grading (grading on a curve) "assumes that the performance of students should approximate the bell curve . . . and forces [student] scores and grades into a normal distribution" (Marzano, 2003, p. 19). Students may begin education with a normal (i.e., bell-shaped) distribution, but at the end of a course, this same distribution reveals that there has been no change, and no observable student learning (Bloom, Hastings, & Madaus, 1991, pp. 52–53).

Norm-referenced grading focuses the student's attention on the teacher's role in awarding grades by a formula, rather than a student's self-directed efforts for learning. Using norm-referenced grading is not a fair practice because "this system produces grades that are unrelated to real achievement" of course competencies (Stiggins, 2005, p. 307). A predetermined and enforced distribution encourages competition among students for the limited number of high grades allowed, diminishing student collaboration, and deterring students from helping one another, which undermines student learning.

One reason for faculty to use norm-referenced grading practices is the disapproval of administrators/peers if too many students in a course earn either high grades or low grades (Walvoord, 2004). Though high grades indicate that a teacher is facilitating student learning, relative grading ensures that "too many" students do not earn high (or low) grades, regardless of instructional effectiveness or student learning. This practice of avoiding too many high or low grades has been termed "defensive marking" (Halpern & Hakel, 2003).

The syllabi of the norm-referenced, work-pace 2 group indicated that "an A is awarded for end of the semester average of 80 percent or more of the total possible points, based on a modified curve of the total points for all exams and assignments." The syllabi for the remaining norm-referenced, work-pace 4 instructional group stated, "Grades will be based on the highest earned points on all required assignments by an individual in the class. Ninety percent of this score equates to a B, 80 percent to a C, etc."

It is improbable that students comprehend their course progress or can predict their grade when norm-referenced practices are the primary grading method. For example, a student in a norm-referenced course may do poorly on most assignments and receive a high score at the end of the course, or do well on most assignments and receive a low score, depending upon how peers perform. Student uncertainty about course performance has been associated with course withdrawal, especially for achievement-oriented students (Nasser & McInerney, 2016).

Varied grading systems used in academics compound the problem of weighting different factors across teachers and students, and even with the same teacher over time (Wiggins, 2014). Instructors themselves express their confusion of standards, accountability, and grading procedures when they claim that high rates of student performance indicate either low course standards or easy grading practices, but not actual student learning (Popham, 2005).

To be credible measures of student learning, grades documented by the registrar need to be supported and interpreted by knowledge of instructional practices including course work-pace and grading procedures. Capturing the course grading practice with work-pace is conceptually reasonable because students experience these instructional practices concurrently.

MEASURING COURSE WORK-PACE

"Many classrooms are set up to treat knowledge as a commodity with the focus on memorizing. Few courses help students build knowledge from personal experiences to make better sense of the world" (Study Group on the Conditions of Excellence in American Higher Education, 1984, p. 15). This philosophy of instruction has changed little over recent decades because college teachers typically use the same methods as their own college professors. Most college teachers have little if any training in how to teach and do not study educational literature outside of their discipline.

Instructional practices that promote student "meaning-making" are encouraged (Fear, Doberneck, Robinson et al., 2003). Building knowledge through meaning-making often requires less content distributed over time. Course workload/pace that allows students the time necessary for distributed learning (rather than "cramming" for examinations) results in deeper learning and student satisfaction. Erring on the side of more depth than breadth is associated with long-term retention. Conceptual understanding is essential for student learning and satisfaction.

Introductory psychology textbooks incorporate history of psychology, research methods and statistics, research detailing brain structures and functions, usual and altered states of consciousness, human development patterns from conception through death, ten or more theories of personality, fifteen or more specific psychological disorders and treatments, chapters on cognitive and social psychology, along with additional subfields within the psychology discipline.

College textbooks have a minimum of a 10th-grade reading level and are densely packed with jargon to deliver the content. Jargon is a term for (often scientific) terminology that has nuanced meaning within a discipline, often different from the commonly understood definition of the word. Instructors who push through every chapter for "coverage" force students to accept a superficial grasp of the content to achieve passing test grades.

An excessively pressured (or lax) course work-pace as reported by students correlates with lower reported learning and higher rates of attrition. Learning requires practicing course content in multiple ways over time. Research on interactions between the learner, the curriculum, and instruction conclude that a suitable amount of information distributed over time is crucial for student learning. A meta-analysis of twenty years of research on teaching reported that amount learned, organization, breadth of coverage, and level of work or difficulty were "factorially invariant" (Theall, 1999, p. 31).

Educational research concludes that student learning is associated with moderate course work-pace that permits time for practice and corrective feedback. Students have a higher rate of learning when instructors cover topics in depth, rather than superficially, and provide numerous and varied opportunities to apply classroom subject matter to new situations and problems. The skill of faculty in challenging and supporting student learning makes a difference in student success (Upcraft et al., 2005, p. 517).

EXPECTED AND UNEXPECTED FINDINGS

The four instructional groups were based upon teacher, text, amount of course content, and grading practices as described in the course syllabi. The four instructional

Table 6.2.   Sex of Student by Instructional Group

Sample Groups	Male	Female	Sample Group Size
Criterion-referenced, work-pace 1	.08	.17	.27
Norm-referenced, work-pace 2	.10	.15	.25
Criterion-referenced, work-pace 3	.09	.16	.24
Norm-referenced, work-pace 4	.09	.16	.24
Totals	36%	64%	100%

groups were sequenced by level of work-pace (from lowest to highest) and catego-
rized by type of grading practice (criterion- or norm-referenced). Table 6.2 shows sex
of the students across the four instructional groups.

   Table 6.2 shows that each instructional group had equivalent numbers of male
and female students, as expected. If one group had substantially more females in the
group, that might explain that group earning higher grades in a social science course.
This was not the case for sex of the students across instructional groups.

   Research with a correlational design permits conclusions about relationships between predictor variables, such as ability of students and their academic outcomes.
Figure 6.1 shows that student ability was equivalently distributed. However, figure
6.1 also shows that the final grades of students were not equally dispersed across the
four instructional groups.

   The analysis revealed that the student ability variable did not make a strong
contribution for student performance or attrition across the four instructional
groups. The student ability variable accounted for less than 1 percent (.007) of the
variability of student outcomes. This is a noteworthy result because national data

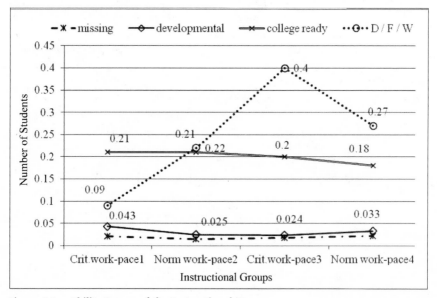

Figure 6.1.   Ability Scores of the Instructional Groups

reports student ACT/SAT scores correlate with student college grade point average (Brookhart, 2015).

The range of specific college entrance test (ACT/SAT) scores could not be used in the analyses, as these measures were not available for a majority of the students in the study. As with the values for ability, males and females were equivalently distributed across the four instructional groups. Discussion of the statistical analyses and tables for the sex and ability variables are located in appendix C.

There was no record whether students in any of the four instructional groups were encouraged to take advantage of the free academic support services provided by the college. No course in the study included an early warning system to identify students at risk for attrition, supplemental instruction, or other intervention. Institutional characteristics were not viewed as factors for variation within the groups, because the data were collected within one institution.

Though sex of the student was significant in the analyses (.007), sex of the student did not emerge as a predictor variable for student performance (A through C-) or attrition (D+ through F and W) in this study. The alpha level ($p < .05$) indicates that these findings could occur by chance in fewer than 1 of 500 trials. The differences in performance and attrition associated with sex or ability of students, while significant, was "a difference so small as to have no practical consequence" (Fraenkel & Wallen, 2006, p. 230).

Ability and sex of student were each significant (each .007, $p < .05$) and together accounted for less than 1 percent (.014) of the variability for student outcomes. The significant findings for ability and sex of the student may reflect the large sample size ($N = 1,614$). The sex and ability levels of students were expected to be evenly distributed across the four instructional groups and were not predicted to influence student outcomes.

For the study of instructional practices and student outcomes, norm-referenced grading practices (i.e., grades based upon the order of student performance) were expected to reflect a more even spread of student scores, regardless of how students clustered, because the cut-off points were evenly distributed across the student scores. Criterion-referenced grading is associated with diverse patterns of student outcomes, and thus varied outcomes were expected for students in courses utilizing this grading method.

An array of instructional methods, variety and frequency of student assessment opportunities with corrective feedback, and forthright grading practices support student success. Appropriate difficulty refers to the amount and pace of course assignments, neither too challenging nor too easy, and is the "salient factor" for student learning, according to correlational and experimental research (Driscol, 2015).

The work-pace of each course was expected to influence student outcomes based on the educational literature. "If you're going to demand excellence, you can set it so nobody can reach it or you can build to it; taking the mystery out of grading and the arbitrariness out of judgment can help build understanding" (Hargreaves, Earl, & Schmidt, 2002, pp. 9–10). Appropriate level of academic challenge continues to be one of the five benchmarks for excellence in education (Dumford, Cogswell, & Miller, 2016).

7

Instructional Practices That Support Student Outcomes

Instructional practices of 60 Introduction to Psychology courses were examined to investigate instructional practices associated with two-year college student outcomes. Variables identified in the records consisted of grading practices (criterion- or norm-referenced); course work-pace (four levels, ranked from lowest to highest); and four levels of grades: 1) As, 2) Bs, 3) Cs, and 4) Ds, F (fail), and W (withdraw).

The literature on grading practices predicts that norm-referenced grading will diminish student outcome differences by assigning grades to the order that students perform, creating an even distribution and obscuring the impact of course work-pace and other instructional variables (O'Connor, 2017). Criterion-referenced grading assigns points with specified course competencies and is predicted to reveal differences in student learning.

GRADING PRACTICE AND WORK-PACE FINDINGS

Diversified student outcomes are shown in figure 7.1, as expected with criterion-referenced practices. The two criterion-referenced, work-pace groups were oppositely skewed, and their combined values equal the norm-referenced groups' combined values. Figure 7.2 portrays the expected similarity between the two norm-referenced groups, despite the extent of the work-pace differences.

Because the predictor variables of criterion-referenced grading and work-pace are negatively correlated, their contribution is undermined within the analyses (Whitley, 2006, p. 243). This result masks the difference of the criterion-referenced instructional groups for student outcomes between one another, and from both norm-referenced instructional groups.

Figure 7.1 reveals the suppression effect within the data and explains the correlations between 55 and 60 percent for the combined grading practice and work-pace

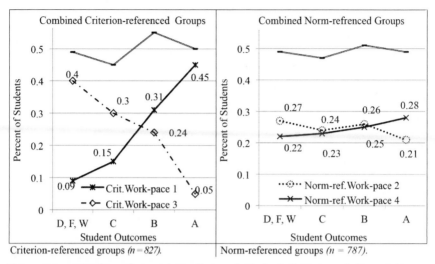

Figure 7.1. Criterion-referenced Grading and Student Outcomes (left) and Norm-referenced Grading and Student Outcomes (right)

instructional factors. This finding demonstrates that student outcomes that rely on college records should be measured at the granular level of students, instructors, and courses because aggregate data can obscure important relationships (Bers & Calhoun, 2004).

Statistical analysis revealed that the type of course grading practice was significantly associated ($p < .001$) with student outcomes. The alpha level (p value) represents the probability that these results could occur less than one in a thousand times. The criterion-referenced grading accounted for more influence than student sex, ability, or norm-referenced grading practices for predicting student outcomes.

Due to the significant finding, a follow-up test was completed to determine where the differences in student outcomes were located. The post hoc tests revealed that students with the highest completion rates were enrolled in the criterion-referenced, work-pace 1 courses. As work-pace increased, performance decreased, and this relationship was more pronounced with criterion-referenced grading practices than with norm-referenced grading practices. These findings confirm previous research that

- norm-referenced grading practices result in predetermined and undifferentiated outcomes (in spite of the highly divergent course work-pace between these instructional groups); and
- rates of attrition are associated with "too high" or "too low" work-pace, though this sample may not have included an instructional group representing a "too low" work-pace.

The opposite skew of the student outcomes for the two criterion-referenced groups explains the suppressed influence of the grading practice variable (.001) when entered into the equation ($p < .001$). Because grading practices were contextualized within the work-pace groups, the effects of grading practices were partially observed in the contribution made by the work-pace variable. Instructional practices of grading and work-pace together accounted for close to 13 percent (.128) of the variation across student outcomes. The combined correlation (.143) for all variables represents a medium effect size ($p < .001$), indicating that slightly more than 14 percent of the variation can be attributed to student sex (.007), ability (.007), and grading practices (.001) integrated with work-pace (.128).

These analyses leave approximately 86 percent of the variability in student outcomes unaccounted for in this study. Unidentified instructional and student characteristics may be stronger predictors of student performance and attrition than course work-pace and grading practices, but were not consistently available in the institutional records for these analyses.

No interaction effects were found in these analyses. Discussion of the statistical assumptions required, analyses, and tables are presented in appendix C.

ENROLLMENT AND ATTRITION

Enrollment was capped at 30 students per course (although instructors had the discretion to allow additional students). Social science courses scheduled between 9 a.m. and 3 p.m. are typically full enrollment courses. However, the number of students enrolled after drop-and-add (or the count date), as well as throughout the semester, resulted in differently sized groups.

Ninety-six students were listed more than once in the data after their initial enrollment because they had taken the course multiple times with one or more of the instructors within the sample over the six-year period. These students were not retained in the data because statistical analysis precluded having the same students in the data set multiple times. Seventy-eight (of the 96 students) reenrolled in the courses with lower work-pace, while 28 reenrolled in the higher work-pace courses.

Thus, removing the students from their second enrollment disproportionately reduced the enrollment totals from the course sections with lower work-pace. Despite this procedure, the lower work-pace groups maintained higher enrollment compared with the higher work-pace instructional groups. The data underscored that more students elected to "retake" the course with a different instructor when their earlier course with the failing grade was in a higher work-pace course, independent of course grading practices.

Consistently lower enrollment/higher attrition as compared with other sections scheduled at the same time indicates the lack of student confidence/satisfaction in specific courses (Noel-Levitz, 2012). The courses in the study consisted of peak enrollment times, with full enrollment on day one of the course—that is, 30 (or more) students each on the rosters. Yet the courses in the study had disparate enrollment within two weeks of the course start dates. Differences in student enrollment and attrition across the instructional groups are portrayed in figure 7.2.

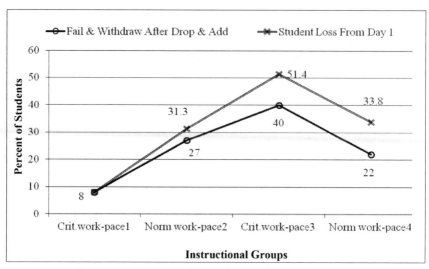

Figure 7.2. Attrition Across Four Instructional Groups

Attrition rates have been used as a measure of the quality of instruction, with the same course taught at the same time by different instructors. Students who are not learning drop courses at a higher rate than students who are learning. The highest enrollment, performance, reenrollment, and lowest attrition were for those courses with lower work-pace across the 60 courses.

Higher enrollment was maintained in lower work-pace courses independent of grading procedures (criterion- or norm-referenced). Criterion-referenced, work-pace 3 and norm-referenced, work-pace 4 groups (highest work-pace groups) had the lowest enrollment, lowest reenrollment, and the highest rates of attrition.

The proportional attrition and reenrollment across the four instructional groups revealed that student "drops" increased as work-pace increased and students re-enrolled to "retake" the course in a lower work-pace course than in their initial, familiar course, when their original course had a higher work-pace. These findings confirm that enrollment, attrition, and reenrollment are aligned and may better predict student performance and hence learning than grades in courses with norm-referenced grading practices.

Student evaluation of instruction (SEI) research concludes that when work-pace is optimal (appropriate challenge with adequate time to learn), performance is high and attrition is low. Following this relationship, the results of the criterion-referenced, work-pace 1 group (with 13 chapters and 300 pages assigned across 15 weeks) appears to have been experienced by students as appropriately challenging with neither "too low" nor "too high" work-pace. The criterion-referenced, work-pace 1 group incorporated ten tests, three papers, and a comprehensive final, while the other groups reported from five to eight tests across the semester.

Scheduling frequent tests encourages students to keep up rather than delaying study, which results in "cramming" a broad amount of information weeks later in the course for an exam. Fewer testing opportunities create higher anxiety and higher stakes, as each test/paper counts for more of the course credit and covers more information. Anxiety diminishes the energy available for test performance.

Consistently higher rates of student enrollment (106 percent), higher performance rates (91 percent passing), and lower rates of student attrition (9 percent) were found in the criterion-referenced, work-pace 1 group. These results are remarkable, considering 11.5 percent of successful students were removed from the criterion-referenced, work-pace 1 group due to their previous enrollment in other instructional groups over the time of the study. Notwithstanding the removal of these students, the criterion-referenced, work-pace 1 group had 30 percent more students enrolling than the other three groups.

Substantial content disparity was documented (186 pages, plus additional pages that were assigned per the course syllabi and not added into the page total) between the norm-referenced, work-pace 4 group over and above the norm-referenced, work-pace 2 group. Yet the difference in student grade outcomes between the two norm-referenced groups was not markedly different.

Both of the norm-referenced instructional groups had the same number of tests (seven), though the norm-referenced, work-pace 4 group also required almost double the reading, plus a research paper, a class presentation, and a comprehensive final examination. Actual student performance scores prior to norm-referenced adjustments remain unknown, so whether the similar performance found between norm-referenced groups indicated comparable learning or similar achievement of course competencies cannot be determined.

Although individual student withdrawal may result from personal circumstances, the rate of student-related reasons for attrition tends to be consistently low across courses. Average attrition has been defined as 14 percent, and a "high-risk" course has been defined as maintaining 30 percent student failure and withdrawal (Bambara, Harbour, Davies, Gray, & Athey, 2009). These "high-risk" guidelines include attrition from physical science courses, known to have higher attrition rates than social science courses.

Corresponding with "average" (14 percent) and "high-risk" (30 percent) definitions, the criterion-referenced, instructional group 2 (with the higher work-pace) could be labeled "high-risk" with an average of 40 percent attrition across 15 courses. The two norm-referenced courses with attrition rates averaging 22 percent and 27 percent respectively, included some courses with 30 percent or higher attrition. The three higher work-pace groups resulted in attrition rates of 22, 27, and 40 percent respectively, and exceeded an average attrition rate of 14 percent.

These results are particularly alarming because 30 percent of college students successfully complete a psychology course in high school, indicating that this introductory psychology course was not the first exposure to the content for approximately one-third of students (Keith, Hammer, Blair-Broeker, & Ernst, 2013). Student enrollment in a high school psychology course was not a variable that was available to be included in this study. Due to the size of the sample, it is expected that those who successfully completed a psychology course in high school were equivalently distributed across the four instructional groups.

SUMMARY OF FINDINGS

This study obtained some measure of the effects of course work-pace and grading practices for student course enrollment, performance, attrition, and reenrollment. While these outcomes were arguably not the same as student learning, these analyses indicated associations between instruction and student outcomes. This study adds to the body of research on instructional work-pace, with the qualification to observe course work-pace in the context of grading practices. The statistical analyses of the institutional data found that

1. Student performance and attrition rates were associated with work-pace requirements for criterion-referenced courses with a medium effect size ($p < .001$).

   (a) Criterion-referenced courses with the lower work-pace (could possibly be described as moderate) were positively correlated with student enrollment, performance, reenrollment, and negatively correlated with attrition.
   (b) Criterion-referenced courses with higher work-pace were negatively correlated for student performance, enrollment, reenrollment, and positively correlated with attrition.

2. Grading practices can modify student outcomes associated with course work-pace:

   (a) Norm-referenced grading suppresses student outcome differences by bundling student grades in a predetermined pattern to prohibit "too many" high or low grades.
   (b) Criterion-referenced grading aligns levels of specified course objectives with points and can reveal student outcomes associated with course work-pace.

3. Despite previous research findings that females earn higher grades than males in social science courses, the variable of sex of student was not a practical predictor (independently or interactively) for student performance (A through C–) or attrition (D+ through Fail and Withdrawal).

4. The operational definition of ability used in this study was limited to "College Ready" or "Developmental" (needs to successfully complete one or more developmental courses prior to enrolling in a college-level course). The dichotomous nature of this measure of ability constrained the full variability of the

ability measure. In each condition students were deemed ready to succeed by completing a needed developmental course or having a college-ready reading, writing, and math score.

Perhaps if each student had a recorded ACT or SAT score, the ability measure might have indicated consequential associations with student performance or attrition. However, the variability of student ability as measured was not a practical predictor (independently or interactively) for student performance or attrition across the instructional groups.

Aggregate data can alter the original characteristics of data or conceal important findings. Combining courses with criterion-referenced grading practices that had different levels of course work-pace suppressed patterns of student performance and attrition in this study, associated with the level of work-pace. Comparing the distributions of student outcomes across the same classes, taught by different instructors, reveals more about instructional practices and student learning in educational contexts than the analyses of aggregate course and program data.

The loss of information in aggregate data is known as the "ecological fallacy" and must be addressed in educational research (Trochim & Donnelly, 2006). This study confirmed that in higher education, institutional data must be nested within the level of courses (indicating grading practices and work-pace) to unravel patterns in student learning outcomes.

In this sample, 80 percent of the students tested as "College Ready" and 13 percent of students successfully completed "Developmental" courses prior to enrolling in the introductory course. The data indicated that students had the ability to succeed in the introductory psychology course at the time of their enrollment.

Though similar percentages of students testing "College Ready" were enrolled in the four instructional practice groups of introductory psychology, these students achieved disparate rates of performance related to the instructional practices they experienced. Twenty-three percent of the "College Ready" group did not successfully complete their first psychology course. Ninety-five percent of these students were enrolled in the two highest work-pace course sections.

Students who were required to successfully complete "Developmental" courses prior to enrolling in college-level courses earned higher grades in the criterion-referenced, work-pace 1 courses. This finding confirms previous educational research regarding optimal work-pace and criterion grading: The "increase in the possibility that all students can succeed . . . and greater student success will be reflected in a greater proportion of higher grades . . . and the positive difference in student performance is even greater for low-achievers" (Stiggins, 2005, p. 306).

These are important findings because students who earn Cs and below in their general education courses are overrepresented in the population of students who do not complete an associate's degree. The First Circuit Court of Appeals ruled that matters such as "course content, workload, and grading policy are core higher education concerns, integral to implementation of policy decisions" (Kaplin & Lee, 2014, p. 307).

Thus, it is imperative that research of best instructional practices regarding course content, workload, and grading policy are communicated to a broad audience of college stakeholders, and that these practices be required to be employed and assessed in two-year colleges.

This study lends empirical support that an optimally challenging work-pace and criterion-referenced grading practices are associated with higher rates of students and institutions achieving their goals. The secret of student performance and retention "is no secret at all. . . . Pedagogy invariably shapes learning" (Tinto, 1997, p. 620).

III

DOES INCREASING STUDENT ACCESS IMPROVE STUDENT SUCCESS?

8

The Continuum of
Instructional Course Designs

Flipped, hybrid, and online courses offer enrollment opportunities for students with extensive out-of-school commitments, lack of reliable transportation, or who live some distance from the college, especially during winter months in places where travel can be precarious. Online courses permit all students to secure a full schedule, when needed face-to-face courses are offered at the same time. Students with physical challenges may prefer online classes if they experience difficulty navigating the college campus.

Offering courses that require less or no seat time with course instruction and assignments that can be managed around other commitments is promoted as increasing student college access. Two-year college student responsibilities often coincide with family and work commitments, and these student characteristics are more evident for those who enroll in online and hybrid courses.

Students enrolled online and in flipped classrooms (also called inverted instruction) receive instruction via viewing video lectures, listening to podcasts, reading, writing, and completing practice tests in an online environment (Bishop & Verlager, 2013). Flipped or inverted course designs are promoted as increasing student learning as compared to other methods of instruction. Class time in a flipped format is used for discussion and student group activities, while the course instruction is assigned outside of class.

Offering courses with less face-to-face class time can be beneficial for students who have extensive work commitments/childcare responsibilities/those in medical/engineering/other technical programs with clinical rotation/apprentice/fieldwork commitments. Both inverted and online formats are considered student-centered modes of instruction because emphasis is placed upon students doing the work of learning, rather than on the teachers' presentation of course content.

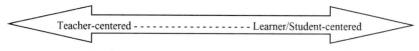

Face-to-face / Traditional ← → Flipped* ← → Hybrid** ← → Online / Distance Education

Teacher responsible for providing instruction with face-to-face lectures, assignments, and feedback. Students responsible for attending class and completing assignments and tests.	Teacher provides instructional guidance and feedback via technology. Student responsible for accessing the instruction and completing assignments and tests independently.

*Flipped: face-to-face time used for activities/labs; instruction takes place outside of class.

**Hybrid: fifty percent of face-to-face class time, instruction takes place outside of class.

Figure 8.1.   Continuum of Instructional Designs

Figure 8.1 portrays a continuum of teacher- to student-centered instruction. Teacher-centered places the emphasis upon what the teacher "is doing, thinking, and talking about and not on the interaction and engagement of students with the core concepts and skills of a course" (Boettcher & Conrad, 2010, p. 7). The traditional lecture-based design exemplifies the teacher disseminating knowledge to students, that is, "professing," and is considered a "teacher-centered" course design. Though the teacher-centered design has been prominent at colleges in the United States, this instructional format is currently losing traction with the advent of online learning technologies.

Student-centered methods have rarely been practiced with large undergraduate face-to-face courses because alternatives to traditional lecturing take more time and more effort for students to complete and for instructors to design and evaluate (Honeycutt, Garrett, & Glova, 2014). Student-centered instruction is often implemented with graduate seminars, where students deconstruct theory and research in their discipline, because lecture as the primary method of instruction is not recommended for deep learning of academic content.

Today, students do not have to depend upon the physical presence of teachers and libraries to find information. Because of the worldwide internet, some educators question whether teacher-centered/lecture-based courses are the best mode of instruction "when students can see the same material covered more authoritatively and engagingly, at their own pace, on their own schedule" (Berrett, 2012, p. 1). Benefits of online instruction include anytime availability of the instructional resources and contact with an instructor/or other students.

Traditional college-age students (18 to 22) often enroll in face-to-face, daytime classes while online students are likely to be older, with work/family responsibilities. When online students are within the traditional age range, they are more likely to have higher rates of (a) full-time work/dependent children or (b) participation in a collegiate sport with a travel schedule than students who enroll in face-to-face classes.

Because online students are not required to be physically present on campus, they tend to be less integrated with the institution and with other college students (Rovai,

2003). Students may need to enroll in flipped, hybrid, or online courses for many reasons. Many of the reasons students need online course opportunities are also the reasons that interfere with completing assignments and learning course content.

These students must generate adequate time and effort around the responsibilities and hardships that prevent them from physical college attendance. However, student outcomes in learner-centered courses suggest that too many of these students underestimate the time, self-discipline, and independent learning necessary for success in these courses. Students in learner-centered courses are more susceptible to procrastination because they do not have the face-to-face physical contact with their teacher and peers each week (Babcock & Marks, 2011).

Regular face-to-face social interaction prompts students to keep up, complete assignments, and ask for help when needed. A lack of face-to-face campus contact may disadvantage online students with accumulated lost opportunities to build relationships with faculty, peers, and college service specialists within the library, computer labs, and counseling and tutoring centers.

Although colleges provide versions of most student services via the internet, having access to the technology and added technological skills are required to make use of these resources. The online services may not approach the level of social engagement experienced by face-to-face students. Student-centered instruction demands self-motivated students to read the text/listen to the audio text, view the lecture/assigned videos, and study and evaluate assigned resources outside of the classroom.

Flipped, hybrid, and online courses require students to have the capability to do most of the work of learning independently, outside of class, in comparison with the direct instruction of much of the course content in face-to-face courses. Those experiencing online instruction have to exert more effort in the "prioritizing and planning" phase, as well as the "practice" phase of self-regulation (shown in figure 8.1), as they navigate a learning management system.

Those in learner-centered courses are often required to describe their understanding of objectives and submit their thoughts to a public course discussion forum. Students may be required to read one another's writing assignments online and to point out inconsistencies and errors in their peers' understanding of the content/ build upon what a peer has argued.

In this way, learner-centered instruction takes advantage of one of the best-known methods of learning: explaining one's understanding to others. This is the converse of a teacher explaining the meaning of the assigned reading to students, evaluating each student's grasp of the subject matter with testing and other assignments, and communicating correct answers for the graded work.

In a face-to-face course, students can raise their hands to ask a question or request more description of a concept. To be successful in student-centered courses students must have knowledge of how and where to find information, evaluate the information, and the self-discipline to do so independently. Essentially, student-centered learning depends upon student self-regulation.

SELF-REGULATION SKILLS

Organizational skills are necessary for students to determine the time they need to commit to learning course objectives depending upon their own background in the discipline. Self-regulation skills encompass the self-discipline to complete quality course assignments by the due dates, track their grades, and contact the teacher with course questions and concerns.

According to Cassidy (2011) and Bjork, Dunlosky, and Kornell (2013), student self-regulation strategies include:

- scheduling study in regular increments over time and using study time effectively;
- deep reading and cogent summarizing of text/video lectures/other assigned sources;
- thoughtful reflection and synthesis of claims, evidence, and credibility of sources;
- anticipating and preparing for examinations, using efficient study strategies.

Teacher-centered instructional designs require less student self-regulation than student-centered designs, because in face-to-face courses teachers often review, emphasizing information to be tested, and remind students of impending assignments and tests. Successful students across instructional designs report that using self-regulated learning strategies accounts for their academic achievement. Self-regulation strategies enable students to exert control over their behavior and environment, to continually ask, "Does this strategy work for me for this task, in this situation?" (Le & Wolfe, 2013).

Figure 8.2 shows how self-regulation is necessary for independent learning (adapted from Zimmerman & Campillo, 2003). The concept of academic self-regulation is related to self-efficacy. Self-efficacy in education is the belief, based upon previous experience, that one can be successful within a given academic domain.

Self-regulation depends upon individuals believing that they can improve their skills through their own efforts; these individuals are described as having a "growth mindset"

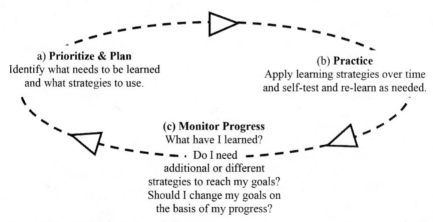

a) Prioritize & Plan
Identify what needs to be learned
and what strategies to use.

(b) **Practice**
Apply learning strategies over time
and self-test and re-learn as needed.

(c) Monitor Progress
What have I learned?
Do I need
additional or different
strategies to reach my goals?
Should I change my goals on
the basis of my progress?

Figure 8.2.   Academic Self-regulation Cycle

(Dweck, 2016). A growth mindset involves an "internal locus of control," that is, accepting responsibility for outcomes. Having an "external locus of control" is the tendency to place blame on others/circumstances/situations that one cannot control and to consider success to be due to luck, or some element outside of personal influence.

Having a growth mindset or an internal locus of control can be practiced and strengthened. Self-regulation, a growth mindset, and internal locus of control are valuable attributes for learning across instructional formats. In a study to identify variables associated with online attrition, gender, age, educational level, previous online experience, occupation, self-efficacy, online learning readiness, prior knowledge, and locus of control were analyzed.

This research concludes that self-efficacy with online technologies, online learning readiness, and previous online experience are statistically significant for successfully completing an online course (Yukselturk, Ozekes, & Turel, 2014). A key difference between instructional designs is that with less (or no) face-to-face contact with teachers and peers, students need more technical skill with academic platforms, and access to technology for online contact with teachers and peers.

TECHNOLOGY AND INTERNET SKILLS

Colleges consistently report that online and hybrid courses have higher student withdrawal and failure rates (Xu & Smith Jaggars, 2013). Student proficiency with the academic learning management system (LMS) is a critical factor for student success in online courses. Examples of LMS include Blackboard, Moodle, Course Canvas, Desire 2 Learn, and others.

Perhaps the higher rates of attrition reflect that students do not have sufficient computer access and are a result of underprepared students/a lack of self-management/ organizational/self-regulation/study skills to devote the time and effort to pass student-centered college courses. Online students tend to have higher rates of risk in terms of needing remedial or developmental courses/having disadvantaged backgrounds, compared to students enrolling in face-to-face courses.

Prior to first online enrollment, many students expect to have the technological knowledge to be successful. Students gauge their technological competence upon their experiences using social media, smartphones, and online gaming activities. However, these technical experiences do not tend to transfer to skill navigating the college's LMS (Pellegrino & Hilton, 2012).

Distance learners must have the skills to negotiate the out-of-class assignments with web-based educational software, find and evaluate required internet sources, and access and navigate publisher software (with its own quirks and glitches). These requirements present an additional barrier to successfully completing a course founded on independent learning. These added requirements present obstacles that may tip the scales toward attrition in flipped, hybrid, or online courses.

Students may believe online courses will be easier than face-to-face courses, because they do not have to go to class. Instead, learning course content is often more difficult for students when they do not have to attend class, because they do not schedule time to learn as they would to attend class. Plus, they may not have adequate experience with the campus LMS/text publisher educational software needed to access instruction, complete, and submit their assignments and tests.

One student likened her online experience to the time she discontinued her gym membership and purchased an exercise video to save money. She found it more difficult to schedule and to complete the video workouts at home, on her own, than going to the exercise classes. Adding to the difficulty of blocking out the time needed to work at home, many students experience frustration with their shared spaces, equipment, and home internet connectivity.

Students expect their teachers to guide them through sequential assignments, prioritizing concepts, unpacking jargon, and explaining course objectives with real-life examples. Assignments need to be communicated verbally and in writing and have specific, measurable, accessible, realistic, time-based, quantity and quality parameters. These expectations remain true for flipped, hybrid, and online courses, except that students are responsible for accessing more of the course content outside of class via internet sources.

College teachers expend a great deal of effort and expertise assembling and creating out-of-class assignments such as document searches, videos, and reading and writing assignments for students to study, evaluate, and apply the information to a given task (Weimer, 2014). Despite these efforts to provide out-of-class instruction, flipped and hybrid courses are not popular with students. "While proponents say flipping is a more effective technique than a traditional lecture, many students chafe at it" (Neshyba, 2014).

Students enrolled in flipped or hybrid courses may object to learning independently, outside of class, because most of their educational experience consists of teacher lecture, that is, being told what they need to memorize for the upcoming test (Hinton, Fischer, & Glennon, 2012).

Although Talbot (2014) endorses flipped instruction, he warns teachers to expect "a nontrivial amount of pushback . . . because students have acclimatized to the lecture model. Changing this model violates their expectations and introduces a lot of uncertainty, and conflict can be a coping mechanism" (p. 15). Some students dislike learner-centered instruction because they cannot passively hide in the back of class, text, surf online, or nap during class (Restad, 2013).

Two-year college students are often unaware of the time, effort, and energy demanded for independent learning and do not carve the necessary study time for online assignments out of their numerous, extracurricular responsibilities and social opportunities. It is paradoxical that undergraduate students "chafe" at independent learning; however, practicing these skills prepares students for college success and lifelong learning (Dunkosky, Rawson, Marsh, Nathan, & Willingham, 2013).

ONLINE PARADOX

To be successful in college, especially in learner-centered courses, students need to continually evaluate their understanding of course objectives, to organize their time effectively to complete quality assignments, and adapt study strategies to remember the course content. Students who enroll in learner-centered courses (such as flipped, hybrid, or online) requiring independent learning may not devote adequate time to completing assignments and learning the content, because it is easier to put off study when faced with demanding work/family/other commitments.

Students enrolled in online courses typically have 50 percent (and higher) attrition compared with those in face-to-face courses (Community College Research Center, 2015). However, for those

> students who are passing an online class, they're earning their way through their course requirements. Maybe they are only squeaking by with 'C's', and, as the research shows, they might have gotten 'B's' in a face-to-face class. But they are racking up credits. Some of them are graduating. (Barshay, 2015, para. 5)

Successful students accurately gauge their available time, understand the time requirements necessary to complete coursework, and arrange their schedules in advance, accordingly. Despite lower completion rates online, those who do succeed in online courses have higher graduation rates than the population of students who complete all their requirements in traditional teacher-centered courses (Shea, 2015).

This higher online student graduation outcome is known as "the online paradox" (Barshay, 2015). Perhaps successful online students have higher graduation rates than those who do not enroll online because they have more options to construct a full schedule of needed courses. Enrolling in fifteen college credits each semester multiplies the probability of completing college credits, certificates, and a degree.

Students who successfully complete online courses are also likely to have strong technology skills and the self-regulation habits of time management, self-discipline, study strategies, and persistence (Yukselturk, Ozekes, & Turel, 2014). These skills transfer across instructional designs and disciplines. Because two-year students may need to enroll in flipped, hybrid, or online courses to construct a full schedule, and because those students who are successful in online courses have higher rates of completion and graduation, it is imperative to conduct research on instructional designs and to delineate practices that support students' success across course designs.

9

Patterns of Student Enrollment across Course Designs

To determine if statistical differences in student outcomes across course designs warranted an intervention, the student outcomes of multiple sections of the various courses were compared. Studies conducted using preexisting data undermine the potential for researcher bias. However, such ex post facto research also prevents randomization of participants or control for variables. Examples of variables that may not be equivalently dispersed across the three course design groups include student age, extent of college experience, employment status, and other student characteristics.

DESCRIPTION OF THE COURSES

The courses in the study include face-to-face, flip-hybrid, and online instructional course designs. Flipped, hybrid, and online courses have less or no in-class seat time. Less class seat time may offer students scheduling benefits that could provide more opportunity for college completion. A flipped or inverted course indicates that the instruction is delivered outside of class with class meetings dedicated to discussion, interactive activities, and group work assignments to practice and apply the information presented outside of class.

A hybrid course indicates that students meet for half of the time of a traditional face-to-face course, with half of course instruction given online. The combination of flipped and hybrid indicates the course meets half the time of a face-to-face course, with much of the instruction occurring outside of the class, and the class meetings dedicated to student activities rather than teacher lecture.

To determine the degree that student completion rates vary across course designs with the same content, taught by the same instructor, the enrollment and final grades of students in the courses were compared. In the case of the flip-hybrid courses investigated, the face-to-face meetings were reduced from four hours (an hour on Monday, Tuesday, Wednesday, and Thursday) to one (two-hour) weekly class meeting.

All sections were the same 15-week, 4-credit Introduction to Psychology course, with the equivalent content (textbook, reading assignments, online open-book multiple-choice tests). The instructor created 16 (each 15-minute) video lectures that were assigned for the flip-hybrid and online courses in lieu of the face-to-face instructor lectures. The video lectures were developed to bring the instruction of the face-to-face courses to the flip-hybrid and online courses. The video lectures consisted of narrated PowerPoint™ with several sentences appearing consecutively on each slide with animated visuals of the verbal content.

Assigning videos outside of class is a recommended pedagogy, especially for under-prepared students, because the videos are available for students to review the content as much as needed, rather than a one-time in-class lecture. Video lectures included animated visuals and diagrams such as brain structures. For face-to-face lectures, the instructor created whiteboard drawings and reviewed transparencies of diagrams.

Assigned video lectures included closed-captioning. However, visual content was not described in the captions of the video lectures. All of the courses in the study provided students with lecture outlines to print, including space for students to write personal notes. There was no data identifying students who printed the notes, added their own personal examples and connections, and reviewed their notes throughout the semester.

Students in all courses were invited to meet with the instructor during office hours, or at a time more convenient to the student, and to e-mail the instructor with course questions and concerns at any time. Records of students meeting with the instructor were not maintained. Students received responses to e-mails within a 24-hour period, including evenings and weekends—typically, within several hours of their e-mail contact. Table 9.1 displays the differences in content delivery, including overlap across course designs, previously portrayed in the Continuum of Course Designs (figure 8.1).

All courses included open-text and open-note online multiple choice tests that could be taken two times, with student answers reported, correct answers not given, and the highest score of the two attempts recorded. The online tests were assigned to

- Motivate students to complete the reading assignment by awarding points;
- Support mastery learning through the self-correction of test responses;
- Encourage students to do their own work, with questions and response choices in random order (different each time a test is opened), with correct answers not provided.

Students were invited to confer with the teacher and other students regarding their concerns about test questions and answers. Discussion is a recommended pedagogy to increase student engagement with course content. Occasionally test points were

Table 9.1. Comparison of Instructional Course Designs

Course Design	Face-to-Face	Flip-Hybrid	Online
Meet	1 hr., 4 days, weekly (4 hrs. total) between	1 hr., 2 days, weekly (2 hrs. total) between	No scheduled class meetings
		11:00 a.m. and 3:00 p.m.	
Content delivery	Lecture 2.5–3 hours over 4 days, outline of lecture notes provided.	Out-of-class weekly video lectures (approx. 1 hour)* partial PowerPoint notes provided.	
Writing/test assignments	Biweekly test short-answer with no text/notes.	Weekly test short-answer with 3 × 5 notecard.	Weekly test (open-book/notes). + weekly 600-word essay over videos & reading, submitted to SafeAssign and Discussion Board.
	+ three papers** over lectures & reading, submitted to SafeAssign.		
Peer engagement	2–3 person group activity 1 hour per week.	Weekly (150+ word) peer essay feedback submitted to Discussion Board.	
Late work	No make-up of group activity points. Short answer tests/ papers accepted up to three weeks with points reduced for late.	No make-up for late essay response points. Late essays accepted up to three weeks, with points reduced.	

*Video lectures and multiple video clips totaling a minimum of one hour each week.
**Papers: 1,200- to 1,500-word length (not counting required references).

added for an individual who offered an explanation that could be considered correct when their response was not specified in the test.

Essays and papers were graded with detailed rubrics that were shared with students. Rubrics are a method of communicating expectations and instructions for an assignment by listing the criteria, or what counts, and describing levels of quality from excellent to poor, indicating how the assignment will be graded. Essay requirements specified in the rubric included addressing content from each reading and video assignment in the discussion board forum. The length of essay, relating information to lived experience, and including references were also specified.

Students were asked to use the rubric to assess their own and their peers' essays. The rubric also served to reduce potential subjectivity of the teacher when evaluating student work.

The rubric describing expectations for peer feedback (called essay responses) included respectful communication, pointing out where a peer needs to make changes to meet the essay rubric, minimum required length of essay response, and bringing something additional from one's own experience into the conversation.

Online students were allowed to submit peer responses within three days following the weekly due date, without losing points. Thereafter, the online peer responses were not graded due to the likelihood that students would not find and read peer comments for their essays from previous weeks. The online peer response assignment was designed to promote discussion, offer student-to-student feedback, and to increase student engagement with course content in the online environment. The rubrics for face-to-face and flip-hybrid papers, online essays, and essay responses are presented in appendices D1 and D2.

The face-to-face and flip-hybrid students completed in-class group work, applying course concepts. Sometimes students were asked to present their work in class. The in-class student groups were composed of two to three students to undermine social loafing. Social loafing often happens in larger-size groups with one or two of the students doing most of the work. Points were earned based on the quality of the group work. Students were not allowed to make up missed in-class group activities. When they did not attend, they lost the group activity points.

Students in all instructional groups were afforded extra-credit opportunities for attending college speakers/other academic events to offset any one-time extenuating circumstance of poor performance. Often those who completed extra credit were already earning an A. Students in all of the instructional designs were allowed to make up essays/papers and tests within a three-week period.

REGISTRATION AND ATTRITION

In all course designs, the course website was opened several weeks before the start date. The entry page included a welcome message and links to the course syllabus. Course syllabi were e-mailed to flip-hybrid and online students two to three weeks in advance of the first day of class. Students were encouraged to purchase the textbook, access the publisher resources, and acclimatize themselves to the course website and college learning management system (LMS) prior to the start date of the course.

The distance courses required knowledge of the college LMS and independent learning and were writing intensive. Those students who reviewed the syllabus/course website and dropped the course had time to enroll in another course, if they determined the time commitment, technical skills, or computer access needed did not correspond with their existing commitments and circumstances.

Students who chose to drop prior to the start date left openings for other students to enroll. Replacement enrollees did not have time to make an informed decision about their technical skills, access to the needed technology, and time requirements to choose to enroll in another course prior to the start of the semester. Unfortunately, some students did not review the syllabus or the course site before week one of the course. These students also did not have time to drop the flip-hybrid or online course in time to enroll in a course more aligned with their needs/expectations.

More online students dropped the online course before the semester started, with consequent higher late enrollment (up to the day the classes began) than with traditional courses. The higher rate of D, F, and W outcomes for late enrollees is thought to be due to students' attempting to cobble a schedule together without knowing how the courses fill their particular degree requirements and other issues related to a last-minute registration.

Perhaps late registration is also an indication of insufficient academic goal–oriented behavior, necessary to be successful in college courses. Educational research recommends that enrollment be concluded at least one week before a college course start date because those who enroll close to the start date have higher rates of attrition (O'Banion, 2012). However, in the comparison of outcomes across course designs study, students could enroll up to day one of the courses and thereafter with instructor permission.

Many studies measure online attrition after the drop-and-add (or count date) period (approximately two weeks into the semester). Courses with online assignments typically have higher attrition than face-to-face courses during this time frame as students new to distance education discover that they have to learn how to use the educational technology and much of the course content simultaneously and independently. There are also technical problems that crop up online and for some, managing these issues may become one obstacle too many.

Thus, comparisons of attrition across course designs should be made using day one enrollment. After the two-week period, student withdrawal is more similar across different course designs. Withdrawal remains slightly higher for online courses, due to the self-discipline required to log in and complete assignments at regular intervals, when it is always possible to put off the work in order to attend to present responsibilities without having to face other students or a teacher in the online class.

The instructional groups compared consisted of four face-to-face sections, five online sections, and five flip-hybrid sections. Each group consisted of 129 students, for a total sample of 387 students. The dissimilar number of courses used to attain equivalent groups is due to divergent patterns of student enrollment across the three course designs. The independent variable of this study was Instructional Design, consisting of three groups: face-to-face, flip-hybrid, and online instruction. Student Outcomes comprised the dependent variable, consisting of the four levels of grades (low to high), listed in table 9.2.

Table 9.2.   Study Variables

Instructional Design	Student Performance
Group 1) Face-to-face;	Level 1) D/F/W;
Group 2) Flip-hybrid;	Level 2) C– to C+;
Group 3) Online.	Level 3) B– to B+;
	Level 4) A– to A.

The course syllabi for all instructional design groups stated that the instructor would notify students and initiate withdrawal if the student did not attend/submit assignments for three or more consecutive weeks, to encourage students to keep up, to monitor their progress, and to protect their academic standing. Students were alerted in the syllabi that if they missed so many assignments that they were likely to fail the course, they would be notified and withdrawn by the instructor.

The college policy indicated that students could self-withdraw any time prior to the last week of the course. Requests for a grade of "incomplete" were honored when students had at least 50 percent of the course work completed and had circumstances warranting additional time to complete the class. Student outcomes across the differing course designs were tallied with the same criterion-referenced grading system, shown in table 9.3.

Table 9.3.   Grading Scale for Instructional Groups

95% of total points and higher = A	65 to 69.9% of total points = C
90 to 94.9% of total points = A–	60 to 64.9% of total points = C–
85 to 89.9% of total points = B+	55 to 59.9% of total points = D+
80 to 84.9% of total points = B	50 to 54.9% of total points = D
75 to 79.9% of total points = B–	45 to 49.9% of total points = D–
70 to 74.9% of total points = C+	Below 44.9% of total points = F

Student-initiated withdraw accepted until final examination week. Teacher initiated withdraw if (a) student missed three consecutive weeks of work and (b) no communications from student regarding extenuating circumstances. From course syllabi.

Final student grades of D, F (fail), and W (withdraw) were collapsed into one category, because there were only several students across the sample groups who earned grades of D or F (fail), because failing students were allowed to withdraw up to the week of final examinations. Combining D, F, and W grades is reasonable because these grades do not transfer across institutions of higher education, or allow students to enroll in upper-level courses in a discipline within the college.

ATTENDANCE AND WITHDRAWAL

The online courses in this study had full enrollment; however, the online roster changed daily in the two weeks prior to the course start date. Online course sections lost more students (approximately 20 percent) in the two weeks until registration was closed. Additional student withdrawal occurred at a higher rate throughout the semester for online courses than in face-to-face courses.

The flip-hybrid courses did not have full enrollment on day one, although the courses were scheduled when there was not another face-to-face course, and at a time when two face-to-face courses would usually have full enrollment. Enrollment patterns coincided with diminished student performance for flip-hybrid courses only. Students appeared to avoid enrolling in hybrid courses at this institution (flipped or otherwise) and to fail at higher rates when not avoided, than students who enrolled in face-to-face or online courses.

Five sections of online courses and five sections of flip-hybrid courses produced an equivalent number of students to compare with four face-to-face courses. Each group had 129 students. The difference in the number of course sections was due to the lower enrollment for flip-hybrid courses, and higher attrition for flip-hybrid and online sections in the first two weeks of the semester. Online students were dropped by the teacher at a higher rate than students enrolled in face-to-face courses or in flip-hybrid courses.

When an online student failed to submit weekly assignments consecutively for three weeks and did not contact the teacher explaining extenuating circumstances, the teacher initiated student withdrawal. The lack of student contact for three or more weeks was construed as the student not attending the online class. When a student struggles to submit an assignment by the weekly due dates, it is unlikely that this student can complete and submit late and concurrent acceptable quality-level assignments over the same time frame.

When students regularly attended face-to-face or flip-hybrid classes and failed to submit assignments/short-answer tests/papers, they were not withdrawn by the teacher. Students who attended class and participated in group activities (equivalent to the weekly peer feedback writing activities assigned to the online students) were able to earn points and remain in their courses.

Students often report that they do not complete reading as assigned or that they complete reading just before a test. Teachers developing flipped or inverted courses are advised to award points for out-of-class work to encourage students to be prepared for the in-class activities/tests. Teachers of flipped and hybrid courses emphasize to students that they must complete reading and other assignments before class to be prepared for the in-class activities.

Students in the flip-hybrid courses typically attended class without having completed the work that would prepare them for the group activity/short answer test. This was apparent by the number of students requesting to complete the weekly short answer test during instructor office hours or at the test center, at a later time/date. It was unusual for students to ask to complete their tests at a later time or day in the face-to-face courses.

As with attendance in face-to-face college classes, some flip-hybrid and online students do not view lectures, submit papers, or prepare for tests. Blackboard™ learning management system (LMS) reports that 30 percent of students in online courses do not view all assigned videos and are not prepared to apply the information in online essays and tests (Firat & Yuzer, 2016).

Many LMSs include analytic technology that reports the time a student is logged into a specific area of the LMS. Blackboard™ analytics indicate that students who are logged in for shorter periods or for longer periods typically do worse in the course, with those students who are logged into the course in the midrange having higher course outcomes.

Due to the review of course records from previous years, the LMS student analytic reports showing when and for how long students were logged into differing features of the courses were not available to analyze. In any event, it may not be reasonable to equate the on-line LMS data of time logged into a course, with flip-hybrid LMS student analytics data and attendance, or with face-to-face student attendance records.

The study indicated that enrollment and attrition patterns differed across the course designs. These differences are significant enough to warrant further investigation. Analysis is needed to develop potential interventions to implement to improve student retention and successful completion for those enrolled in learner-centered course designs. Statistical tables and a discussion of the analyses of the comparison of the three instructional designs are presented in appendix D3.

10

Improving Student Access and Learning Outcomes

Institutional records can be used to investigate instructional practices. Student outcomes from face-to-face, flip-hybrid, and online courses were compared to investigate student completion rates across course designs. Student outcomes were measured with four levels of the final grades: As, Bs, Cs, and Ds or F (fail) or W (withdraw). Course syllabi for all of the courses reported that criterion-referenced grading was used to score student work.

Course outcomes based upon criterion-referenced grading are not expected to have bell-shaped grade distributions, because this method of grading reveals differences in student attainment of course competencies. Figure 10.1 illustrates the

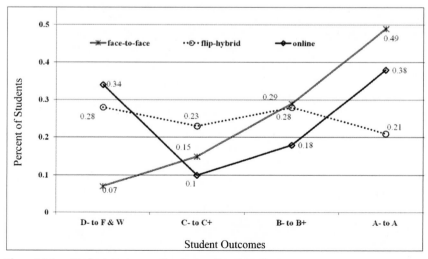

Figure10.1. Student Outcomes for Instructional Designs

absence of "bell-shaped" distributions of student grades across the course designs. A bell-shaped distribution indicates few students earning As, most students earning Bs and Cs, and few students earning grades of D, F, or W.

Grades of students enrolled in the face-to-face courses formed a skewed-linear pattern with many students earning high grades. Students in flip-hybrid courses generated a flat distribution of grades, while the grade frequency of online students was an inverted curve exhibiting few average final grades. Figure 10.1 shows the higher student performance in the face-to-face courses, with fewer students earning Ds, Fs, or Ws than in the flip-hybrid or online courses.

DISCUSSION OF STUDENT OUTCOMES

Students enrolled in the flip-hybrid courses appeared to struggle with out-of-class course assignments, evidenced with fewer flip-hybrid students earning As and Bs than students who completed online or face-to-face courses. Each of the short (three to five pages) papers assigned in the face-to-face and flip-hybrid classes required students to communicate how course concepts were relevant and relatable to their life experiences. Relating course content to lived experience was routine for in-class discussion in face-to-face and flip-hybrid courses. Relating course content to lived experience was also an objective for the online essays and essay responses.

Online students expected to use technology to access and submit course assignments, and online students managed to complete assignments by the due dates or they withdrew before the end of the course. Some students in the flip-hybrid courses appeared resentful of the online course instruction and assignments. All course designs included online open-book, multiple choice tests for course points that were assigned to motivate students to read the textbook each week. Students in flip-hybrid and face-to-face courses needed to be reminded weekly to complete these tests.

The online video lectures, interactive exercises, and video clips were available daily, around the clock for flip-hybrid and online students. The opportunity to review the content as much as needed to learn the information was intended to assist student performance. Yet when direct instruction was shifted out of the classroom for these two-year college students, performance declined in comparison with the traditional teacher-centered courses, with specifically more Ds, Fs, and Ws for students enrolled in flip-hybrid and online courses as observed in figure 10.1.

It is notable that Ds and Fs were collapsed with W grades because there were so few Ds or Fs in the course final grades. Most of the those in the DFW category resulted from course withdrawal, whether student or teacher generated, prior to the final examination week. The student outcomes for those in teacher-centered courses indicate that students who regularly attended the face-to-face courses were able to successfully complete enough assignments and tests to pass the course, even if they performed poorly on one or more tests, or failed to submit all of the short papers.

Statistical analyses were conducted for nonparametric (not bell-shaped) data. These analyses revealed significant differences between the three instructional groups. Consequently, follow-up tests were completed to identify where the statistically significant differences between student grade outcomes were located between the three instructional design groups.

Statistical significance ($p < .001$) means that these results are unlikely to occur by chance 1 in 1,000 times and are likely to be real and observable differences. The following differences were obtained:

- The number of students earning grades of A was significantly higher in face-to-face courses compared with those earning As in flip-hybrid or online courses;
- The number of students earning grades of C was significantly higher in flip-hybrid courses compared with those earning Cs in online courses;
- The number of students receiving D, F, or W grade outcomes was significantly lower in face-to-face courses compared with those receiving D, F, or W grades in flip-hybrid or online courses.

There were no significant differences for students earning B grades across the three course designs. Due to the statistical requirement for homogeneity of variance (similar, narrow pattern across the groups) not being met, the results of the analyses should be viewed with caution.

According to Coe (2002), "Effect size quantifies the size of the difference between groups, and may . . . be a true(r) measure of the difference" (p. 3). Effect sizes across groups for grades of D, F, or W were calculated as $d = .07$; Cs comprised $d = .05$, and grades of A resulted in $d = .14$. These findings constitute medium to large effect sizes, described as "visibly perceptible influence" (Cohen, 1994, per Gliner & Morgan, 2000, p. 178).

Though effect sizes imply causality, correlational research such as this shows associations between course design and student learning outcomes. The complete statistical assumptions, analyses, and tables of results for this study are presented and discussed in appendix D3.

PATTERNS OF STUDENT FEEDBACK

Student evaluation of instruction (SEI) research concludes that those in student-centered course designs may resent the lack of direct instruction (Pascarella, Seifert, & Whitt, 2008). Implementing student-centered learning provokes student opposition and resentment associated with student perceptions of appropriate educational activities; that is, "I am not paying tuition to teach myself" (Nilson, 2013). Regarding student evaluations in a flipped course, Berrett (2014) reported:

Many students have done well receiving information and spitting it back out. While some come to embrace the flipped classroom, others never do. . . . The average score on a student evaluation of a flipped course is about half what the same professor gets when using the traditional lecture. (p. 5)

Student evaluations were not required in every face-to-face course, and a minority of students submitted electronic evaluations for their online or flip-hybrid courses. Low student course evaluation participation constituted a small and nonrepresentative sample across courses and between instructional designs. Thus, SEI comments offer little but anecdotal information:

- Face-to-face students commented that they found the psychology course content interesting. They reported that they did not have to struggle in the course and that they would take another course with the teacher.
- The online students who submitted course evaluations reported satisfaction with the course and their learning, for the most part similar to students in traditional courses. Students enrolled in online courses often reported that making and staying on a schedule and getting the reading and writing done each week was difficult, but that they felt that they learned and would take another online course with the teacher.
- The flip-hybrid student responses were split between those who were dissatisfied with the instructional methods and would not take another course with the teacher and those students who were satisfied with the course, their learning in the course, and would take another course with the teacher.

Due to the poor flip-hybrid student evaluations (compared to face-to-face and online student evaluations), the instructor did not teach this course in the flip-hybrid format for a third semester. When a decision to compare student outcomes across the course designs was made, the lack of a larger flip-hybrid sample (n = 129) limited the total sample size, to maintain equivalent size groups for each instructional design.

The large discrepancy in D, F, W grades across the three instructional designs was a factor in the unequal numbers of student evaluations submitted across the course designs because those who withdraw are less likely to submit evaluations of instruction at the end of the course. However, there is no way to attribute the grade earned by a student with the student evaluation of instruction submitted by the student.

IMPROVING STUDENT-CENTERED
COURSE LEARNING AND COMPLETION

The comparison of student outcomes across the continuum of course designs indicated higher early withdrawal and lower rates of completion for courses requiring more independent learning and technology skills. These results suggest that attrition in learner-centered two-year college courses warrants the development and implementation of institution-wide intervention. Interventions must be studied to determine whether completion rates improve, and if so, how the improvement was effected. Educational investment must always show a viable ratio of cost for the value of the benefit.

Aggregate outcomes of those in learner-centered courses oblige educators to screen students prior to allowing them to enroll in courses with these instructional designs. Students who do not successfully complete the screening tasks can be encouraged to access free online tutorials. Students in learner-centered courses need to

- be oriented to online technologies, including how to navigate the campus's learning management system (whether Blackboard™, Canvas™, Desire2Learn™, or another LMS);
- know where to locate assignments online, and how to submit work to LMS Discussion Boards and SafeAssign™ (or other plagiarism-checking software). Students may need proficiency with wikis, journals, blogs, interactive testing (with and without browser lockdowns), and other web-based technologies.
- know how to access and download software to view assigned videos and to complete interactive assignments, simulations, and other online procedures.
- know how to purchase and access publisher resources (embedded in the LMS or otherwise); and where and how to seek help, when (not if) they experience technical problems. (CCRC, 2015)

Unsuccessful students in learner-centered courses might come to believe they do not have the ability to earn college credits, when they could complete their coursework in a face-to-face course and if they acquired technical skills to navigate the college LMS and practiced efficient study strategies. Two-year college students (especially those who are underprepared) are sometimes unaware that they do not know or practice effective study strategies.

The LMS purchased by a two-year college should provide professional tutorials for students and for teachers who use the LMS. Creating the tutorial modules should not be the responsibility of individual teachers or schools. Teacher- and institution-developed LMS tutorials would likely have lower production values than those created by the LMS provider. Tutorials created outside of the LMS provider have the potential to compromise the universality of the LMS across courses and between institutions.

Teachers are encouraged to provide checklists of assignments and due dates so students have the information they need to organize their schedules. Students need to determine how much time to devote to a given assignment depending upon their own reading, writing, technological expertise, background in the subject, and competing commitments. The family/work/athletic/other commitments that prohibit students from enrolling in face-to-face course sections may also interfere with student ability to dedicate the time and effort necessary to be successful in the more isolated and independent, learner-centered course designs.

To increase student success in learner-centered courses, free online orientation tutorials outlining independent learning, time management, and the technology access and skills necessary to be successful are critical. An orientation for flipped/hybrid/online courses should be provided. This orientation should include assignments that require a student to break an assignment down into component parts and to create a reasonable schedule to complete each portion of the assignment, as one indication of student self-regulation.

Online orientations and tutorials need to guide students through specific learning practices, such as organizing the information, relating information to their own experience, and self-testing to convey how to identify objectives that need ongoing study. Students need training in creating study aids such as personalized mnemonics (a diagram, or a sentence, word, or song to remember information).

Examples of mnemonics include "every good boy does fine" (musical notes) and "Roy G Biv" (color spectrum). Mnemonics require time and effort to develop and are an effective method for learning. Students should be required to successfully complete a test of the online orientation competencies, including submitting practice assignments in the LMS, prior to enrolling in their first online or other learner-centered course requiring LMS use.

When specific technology skills are necessary for students to be successful, students should be screened and offered tutorials in these skills, prior to allowing them to enroll in the course. Students experience frustration attempting to learn the educational technology while also struggling to learn the course content. These students withdraw or fail at higher rates than students who have the LMS navigation skills.

Attrition is costly for students who have invested time in school when they could have been earning an income, as well as costly for communities, states, and the federal government that cover much of the expense of higher education. Two-thirds of the students who default on their federal loans are those who withdraw from college. These students may intend to complete college, but their goals are precluded when they shoulder minimum-wage work and student loan payments.

The nature of independent learning demands more of each student and poses more risk of attrition, especially for those students who are academically unprepared. Students can be coached to increase self-regulated learning skills with online tutorials. Those who cannot successfully complete the orientation test could access free online tutorials for the opportunity to practice the skills, then retake the online orientation test prior to being allowed to enroll in their first flipped, hybrid, or online class.

Students who are unsuccessful with the web-based tutorials are likely to fail a learner-centered course, forfeiting time and financial investment without earning college credit. This circumstance is exacerbated when financial aid is exhausted and student loans must be repaid by students with few college credits earned.

Specific kinds of tutorial content such as student interviews, practice assignments, and animation needs to be designed and assessed to identify the tutorials associated with student retention and success in courses that demand extensive independent/

online learning. Requiring first-time, online students to complete an online orientation and test might initially decrease learner-centered enrollments limiting college access, when students cannot enroll in face-to-face courses due to schedule conflicts, lack of transportation, or another impediment.

Learner-centered instruction has been promoted for students due to the growth of open access to information and the necessity of lifelong learning in contemporary society. Because of our ever-evolving technology, citizens need independent learning skills to evaluate the credibility of sources and the quality of information accessed, in order to be successful at school, at work, and in personal life.

Technological advances such as the availability of instructional videos and simulations can support student learning and even be substituted for face-to-face lectures and labs for those students who have sufficient technological and independent learning skills. The gains for students with successful experience in learner-centered courses are reflected in the "online paradox."

Specifically, that in spite of online courses resulting in lower retention, those students who do complete in an online environment have higher rates of college graduation. Furthermore, students who are successful in learner-centered courses are positioned for lifelong learning. Thus, educational literature recommends that college students have some experience with flipped, hybrid, online, or other learner-centered course designs.

Not all adults have the drive or the capability to earn a college degree. Yet individual and family health and well-being are affiliated with college graduation. It is likely that more than a quarter of our citizens (approximate population of college-educated) can benefit from earning a degree. Thus, increasing college access and completion rates is a worthy goal. Economists conclude that if the educational attainment of students in the United States could be raised to the graduation rates of our Canadian neighbors, real wages would increase by 20 percent (Hanushek & Rivkin, 2010).

Providing tutorials that guide students through their use of the academic technology, teach efficient study strategies, and break down assignments into manageable portions has promise of raising completion rates in student-centered courses comparable with face-to-face course completion rates. Perhaps these tutorials could raise face-to-face course completion rates as well. The "online paradox" is a strong indicator that self-regulation and academic technology skills transfer across instructional designs and position students for college completion and lifelong learning (Hu & Driscoll, 2013).

Training and tests should be monitored to verify what kinds and level of intervention increase retention and graduation for specific groups of students. Educators must conduct research to identify instructional practices correlated with student learning, retention, and completion. Effective instructional and institutional practices must be implemented to support student and institutional goals. College access does not confer benefits when students are not provided with the tools and scheduling needed to earn a college degree.

Lifelong learning is recognized as a necessary skill for personal and professional growth because of the high rate of technological change in our culture. Citizens may need to return to formal education multiple times across their careers. Today, knowing how to learn, what to do to learn, and why course content is relevant for the learner, must be at the heart of two-year college curriculums for the benefit of our students and their families, our colleges, our communities, and our country.

Appendixes

Appendix A

Systems Used to Determine Student Ability

Table A.1. Planning and Placement Test Codes Plan

Testing Fall 2003 and after (034).	Testing Fall 2003 and previously (033).
5A = ENG 101	1E = ENG 085 or 089 and RDG 040C
4B = ENG 091	2D = ENG 091 or 085 or 089 and RDG 040A or RDG 040C
3C = ENG 085	3C = ENG
	4B = ENG
	5A = ENG
	OR = RDG 040A with or before ENG 101. Pass with C or better to take general education class. English placement is mandatory.
1A = MATH 040	
2B = MATH 050, 107	
3C = MATH 109, 105, 115, or 151	01 = failed MATH 035 module
4D = MATH 111	
5E = MATH 112	02 = passed MATH 035 module
6F = MATH 161	

7G = MATH 162 Math placement is advisory.
Must earn a grade of C or better in prerequisite math class in order to advance.

10 READCH = reading comprehension at 10th-grade level
10 READVC = reading vocabulary at 10th-grade level

01 = failed Introduction to Computers   02 = passed Introduction to Computers

01 High School Profile – must take English and Reading placement tests
02 High School Profile – waive English and Reading placement tests
22 (or above) ACT – waive English and Reading placement tests, may begin with English 101.

(Business course requirements not included in this presentation.)

The Placement Test Codes Plan was commonly used by community colleges referring to ACT, SAT, and ASSET (placement test developed by American College Testing Services) test scores for an indication of the ability of incoming students to successfully complete college-level coursework (U.S. Department of Education, 2015). Table A.2. ACT and SAT labeled Entrance Tests. SAT scores transformed into ACT scores.

Table A.2. Ability Conversion Formula for Student Entrance Test Scores

Ability	HSP (State High School Profile Test Score)	ASSET (Test for Placement in College-Level Courses)	Entrance tests (SAT Converted to ACT Scores)	Total Students in Each Group
0 = Developmental*	01	1, 2, 3	11–21	202 (12.5%)
1 = College Ready	02	4 and 5	22–34	1,288 (80%)
No score	—	—	—	124 (7.5%)
Total				1,614 (100%)

*Requires one or more developmental courses prior to enrolling in college-level course.

Appendix B1

Criterion-Referenced, Work-Pace 1 Syllabus

Table B1.1. **Assignments and Course Grading**

Assigned reading: Chapters 1–3, 5–7, 10, 12–16.	**Total points = 300**
Tests: 10 tests (each 15 pts.) = 150 points.	95% + of 300 = A
Group activities 10 in-class (each 3 pts.) = 30 points.	90–94.5% = A-
Writing assignments 3 (each 15 pts.) = 45 points.	85–89.5 = B+
Attendance (1 pt. per day without group activities/tests) = 35 points.	80–84.5% = B
Final cumulative exam = 40 points.	75–79.5% = B-
	70–74.5% = C+
Practice tests posted online for each test (except final).	65–69.5% = C
Correct & keep actual tests for final exam study.	60–64.5% = C-
Rubrics for each writing assignment posted online.	55–59.5% = D+
Extra credit available on each examination, if taken with class.	50–54.5% = D
Attendance: Attendance is required.	45–49.5% = D-
(Losing attendance/group activity points can drop your grade.)	below 44.5% = W

Appendix B2

Norm-Referenced, Work-Pace 2 Syllabus

Assigned Reading: Appendix A + text chap. 1–8, 11, 13, 14 + 7 supplemental articles. Tests: seven tests, none cumulative.

Course grading: To provide some motivation for you to read over the assigned chapter(s) before we start our class discussion, you will have an opportunity to complete a brief online quiz prior to the start of each unit. If at the end of the term your quiz scores average 75% or more, you earn 12 extra credit points. If your scores average 60–74% you earn 6 extra-credit points. A missed or incomplete quiz counts as a zero. I will give you a separate handout with instructions for how to log in and take the quizzes.

Final grade will be based primarily on a modified curve of the total points for all exams and assignments, if any. An A is awarded for an end-of-the-semester average of 80% or more of the total possible points, based on a modified curve of the total points for all exams and assignments. I will explain this further during the first class. Class participation will influence whether a "borderline" final grade goes up or down.

There are no make-up exams for any reason.

At the end of the term, the lowest exam score will be dropped (cannot be the last test). If you miss an exam, that one will count as lowest score.

Two missed exams mean an automatic F for the term, unless there are EXTREMELY extenuating circumstances and your other test scores average B or better and you have missed no more than two other classes.

If the assignment is not completed satisfactorily your final course grade will be two full grades lower than your test average. (For example, a test average of B+ would yield a final grade of D+.)

Attendance: Attendance will be taken at every class. Regarding late arrival or early departure, there is a 10-minute grace period at the start or end of each class. After that, each hour or fraction thereof counts as ½ absence. However, if the grace period is abused you will be charged with 2 absences. At the end of the term, assuming your classroom behavior has been appropriate (i.e., no reading magazines, doing math homework, leaving to talk on the phone, sleeping, regularly antagonizing the instructor, etc.), attendance will be graded as follows.

Table B2.1. Attendance Affects Your Grade as Follows:

0–½ absences = up ⅓ grade (e.g., B to B+);
1–1½ absences = no change;
2 absences = down ⅓ grade;
2½ absences = down ⅔ grade;
3 absences = down 1 full grade;
more than 3 absences = don't even think about it.

Appendix B3

Criterion-Referenced, Work-Pace 3 Syllabus

Text, text reading assignments, and tests: To keep you focused and on task, read the weekly chapter assignments prior to class discussion. To get a firm grasp of the material YOU WILL NEED TO READ THE CHAPTERS MORE THAN ONCE.

Table B3.1. Assignments, Testing, and Grading

Assigned reading: Appendix A + Chapters 1–15	1,180–1,062 = A
Tests: 4 quizzes + comprehensive final exam	1,061–944 = B
4 quizzes = 400 points	943–826 = C
1 final exam = 300 points	825–708 = D
20 worksheets/class activities = 480 points	below 707 = F

Papers are expected AT THE BEGINNING OF THE CLASS PERIOD ON THE DATE ASSIGNED. Any paper that is late—for any reason—will be accepted with a five-point penalty. Failure to turn in an assignment will result in zero points on the point sheet. Missed quizzes may be made up at the instructor's discretion and convenience.

Students with at least a 90% average on the four in-class quizzes AND 792 points prior to the final exam will be excused from taking the final and will be awarded an A for the course. The final comprehensive exam including the 15 chapters and the appendix chapter on statistics will be taken by students with less than 792 points prior to the final exam.

Attendance: ATTEND ALL CLASSES! Daily attendance WILL be taken. In the event of illness or other essential absence, STUDENTS ARE RESPONSIBLE FOR CONTACTING THE INSTRUCTOR, UPON RETURN TO CLASS, to see what was missed, and making up the work. After three absences, the student may be called in to explain the reason for the absences and may be dropped from the class. Three (3) tardys [sic] are equal to one absence.

Appendix B4

Norm-Referenced,
Work-Pace 4 Syllabus

Reading assignments: Text prologue, chapters 1–18. A collection of articles is also assigned. [Author note: Articles/page numbers for articles NOT listed in the syllabus.] Tests: seven tests and one cumulative final examination. Research papers will be due on dates coinciding with the student's presentation date.

As a general policy there will be NO make-up work (including tests) for assignments missed during the semester. Most homework and in-class assignments cannot be made up. When there are extenuating circumstances, the student should discuss with the instructor a possible variance of this policy. This should be done outside of class time. Variance from this policy will be solely at the discretion of the instructor and will be more possible when requested before the assignment is due or the test is administered.

Course grading: Final course grades will be based on the following:

1. The six highest test grades earned during the semester (100 points each test).
2. Score on comprehensive final exam (200 points).
3. Quizzes, out-of-class assignments, class participation.
4. APA-formatted research paper (100 points) and in-class group presentation (50 points).

Grades will be based on the highest earned points on all required assignments by an individual in the psychology class. Ninety percent of this score equates to an A, 80 percent to a B, etc. Based on that student's total points, letter grades will be based on the following percentages of the student's points:

Appendix B4

Table B4.1.   Grade Scale

A = 90% or above
B = 80–89%
C = 65–79%
D = 50–64%
F = 0–49%

Attendance: Attend ALL scheduled classes. Attendance will be taken regularly. The student is responsible for all that is done in class should absences occur. A STUDENT MISSING MORE THAN FIVE (5) HOURS (NOT DAYS) OF CLASS WORK WILL BE SUBJECT TO WITHDRAWAL AT THE DISCRETION OF THE INSTRUCTOR. It is the student's responsibility to request a variance of this policy due to extenuating circumstances.

Appendix C

Instructional Practices and Student Outcome Statistical Discussion and Tables

Analyses completed for this study included descriptive statistics to capture the participant and instructional characteristics with linear and logistic multiple regression to identify correlations between type of course grading practices and work-pace, associated with student performance (A through C-) and attrition (D+ through F and W). Multiple regression correlation (MRC) is preferable to analysis of variance (ANOVA) techniques with correlational research, because ANOVA requires groups to be equal while MRC does not, although MRC usually yields identical conclusions to ANOVA.

This data presents an example of the ecological fallacy: a "problem that can arise from the use of aggregate data" when individual or group-level data are combined in a way that alters the original characteristics of the data set (Whitley, 2002, p. 329). One method of checking for this is to look for multicollinearity between predictor variables that can result from "multiple measures of one construct in the set of predictor variables" (Whitley, 2006).

Bordens and Abbott (2004) stated that high correlations between predictor variables mean that the "variables are measuring essentially the same thing, so little is lost by eliminating one of them" (p. 429). To offset this potential problem, it is recommended to combine multicollinear variables into one variable for multiple regression analyses (Norusis, 2015).

The correlation matrix for the variables indicated that the four instructional work-pace groups and the two grading practices exhibited correlations from 55 to 60 percent. Variable correlations that do not exceed 80 percent are considered acceptable for MRC analysis (Whitley, 2006). From the sample of 1,614 students, 787 (49 percent) were in the norm-referenced category while 827 (51 percent) of the students were in the criterion-referenced category. When the data were combined in this way, the work-pace variable was undermined. The variable of criterion- or norm-referencing was subsumed within the work-pace variable.

REGRESSION RESULTS

The *F* ratio/statistic was completed for linear regression with linear patterns. The Wald statistic, "the square of the ratio of the coefficient to its standard error," was completed for logistic regression with linear patterns (Morgan, Gliner, & Harmon, 2001, p. 95). All analyses were completed at a conservative ($p < .001$) confidence level. The goal for the statistical analysis was to determine associations or variations between instructional groups, differentiated by type of course grading practices, course work-pace, and student outcomes.

(*R*) multiple correlation coefficients, a measure of the degree of association between variables; (R^2) correlations of determination, a measure of the portion of the variance; (ß) regression coefficients; and (ΔR^2) the change in the squared multiple regression coefficient were examined to determine patterns of student outcomes brought about by specified changes in the predictor variables of work-pace combined with grading practice.

Due to the ordinal nature of the work-pace variable, dummy-coded vectors were used to differentiate the four instructional groups, ranked from lowest to highest levels of work-pace. A hierarchical regression was completed to access a comparison of influence of each of the four variables (sex, ability, grading practice, work-pace) associated with the two attrition outcomes (successfully completed or not successfully completed).

The analyses revealed the following regression equation:

Student attrition = –4.63 – .27 *(sex)* + .62 *(ability)* + .92 *(grading practice)* – 2.0 *(work-pace group 1)* – .34 *(work-pace group 2)*

Logistic regression determines the likelihood that a particular student was a member of one of the two categories: successfully completed the course rather than did not successfully complete the course. The type of course grading practice was significantly associated ($p < .001$) with student performance and attrition. The logistic analysis for attrition is shown in table C.1.

Table C.1 shows that the Nagelkerke R^2 of .126 for all predictor variables was more than 12 percent of the variance of student attrition could be predicted by sex of the student, ability of the student, and the grading practice and work-pace of the course. Step 3 of the regression analysis revealed that entering the grading practice variable with the four groups collapsed into two categorical groups (criterion-referenced or norm-referenced) had little effect in the equation, with no change in the Nagelkerke R^2.

Step 4 of the logistic regression analysis revealed that the work-pace values produced the strongest influence with a Nagelkerke R^2 change of .116, accounting for more than 11 percent of the likelihood that a student would be located in the "successfully completed" introductory psychology (performance) or "did not successfully complete" (attrition).

Table C.1.   Logistic Regression for Student Attrition (N = 1,614)

Predictor Variable	B	SE	Wald
Block 1			
Sex of student	−.27	.12	4.73 **
Block 2			
Student ability score	.62	.18	12.28***
Block 3			
Grading practice	.92	.16	31.80***
Block 4			
Crit.-ref., work-pace 1	2.00	.20	100.82***
Norm-ref., work-pace 2	−.34	.17	4.20
Crit.-ref., work-pace 3	****	****	****
Norm-ref., work-pace 4	****	****	****

Note. Block 1 (sex) Nagelkerke R^2 = .006; Block 2 (ability) Nagelkerke R^2 = .011; Block 3 (grading practice) Nagelkerke R^2 = .011; Block 4 (work-pace groups) Nagelkerke R^2 = .126.

*p > .05; **p < .05; ***p < .001.
****automatically excluded value from the analysis, as redundant.

Ninety percent of the total influence of the four variables are accounted for by the work-pace variable. According to this analysis, students experienced differential patterns of attrition associated with work-pace requirements that could not be expected to occur by chance. This analysis reveals that course work-pace is associated with student attrition.

Due to the statistically significant results of the analyses, follow-up tests were conducted. Morgan, Gliner, and Harmon (2001) advised the use of Tukey HSD when a multiple regression analysis revealed that the Levene's test was not significant. The Tukey HSD is reported as a robust statistic for comparisons of group means (Norusis, 2015). The follow-up or post hoc test for attrition by instructional groups is presented in table C.2.

Table C.2.   Post Hoc Test for Attrition by Instructional Group (N = 1,614)

Grading Practice, Work-Pace	Mean Difference	Std. Error
Crit.-ref., work-pace 1		
Norm-ref., work-pace 2	.19	.03**
Crit.-ref., work-pace 3	.32	.03**
Norm-ref., work-pace 4	.16	.03**
Norm-ref., work-pace 2		
Crit.-ref., work-pace 3	.12	.03**
Norm-ref., work-pace 4	.05	.03*
Crit.-ref., work-pace 3		
Norm-ref., work-pace 4	.18	.03**
Norm-ref., work-pace 4	***	***

Tukey HSD. *p > .05; **p < .001. ***Noted in preceding rows.

Similar to the hierarchical regression for attrition outcomes, an analysis was conducted to access a comparison of influence of each of the four variables (sex, ability, grading practice, work-pace) associated with the performance outcomes (successfully completed or not successfully completed). This analysis is presented in table C.3.

Table C.3. Linear Regression for Student Performance (N = 1,614)

Predictor Variable	SE	B	t	ß
Step 1				
Sex of student	−.20	.07	−3.02	−.07**
Step 2				
Ability score	.45	.09	4.70	.12***
Step 3				
Grading practice	−.67	.09	−7.50	.32***
Step 4				
Crit.-ref., work-pace 1	****	****	****	****
Norm-ref., work-pace 2	−.15	.09	−1.70	.05*
Crit.-ref., work-pace 3	−1.37	.09	−15.31	−.42***
Norm-ref., work-pace 4	****	****	****	****

Step 1 (sex) R = .085, R^2 = .007; Step 2 (ability) R = .118, R^2 = .014, ΔR^2 = .007; Step 3 (grading practice) R = .124, R^2 = .015, ΔR^2 = .001; Step 4 (work-pace vectors) R = .377, R^2 = .142, ΔR^2 = .127. *p > .05; **p = .003; ***p < .001. ****Values automatically excluded from the analysis as redundant.

Table C.3 shows (analogous to results of instructional practices for attrition) that sex of student negligibly influenced student outcome (R^2 *change of* .007) as did student ability (R^2 change of .007), and grading practice (R^2 *change of* .001) as operationalized in this analysis. The work-pace groups exhibited the strongest significant influence (p < .001) within this study with (R^2 change of .127) a medium effect size for behavioral research according to Cohen (1988). Due to the significant findings a post hoc test was completed to determine specific location of the differences. The post hoc results are presented in table C.4.

Table C.4. Post Hoc Test for Performance by Work-Pace (N = 1,614)

Grading Practice, Work-Pace	Mean Difference	Std. Error
Crit.-ref., work-pace 1		
Norm-ref., work-pace 2	.80	.09**
Crit.-ref., work-pace 3	1.35	.09**
Norm-ref., work-pace 4	.68	.09**
Norm-ref., work-pace 2		
Crit.-ref., work-pace 3	.55	.09**
Norm-ref., work-pace 4	−.12	.09*
Crit.-ref., work-pace 3		
Norm-ref., work-pace 4	.67	.09**
Norm-ref., work-pace 4	***	***

Tukey HSD. *p > .05; **p < .001. ***Calculations noted in preceding rows.

INTERACTION EFFECTS

All of the study variables were tested for possible interactions because educational literature suggests that student and instructional variables have an interactive effect for student performance and attrition. Ability levels and sex of the student were not significantly different across the four instructional groups and interaction for *sex and ability* was determined to be zero with neither variable directly nor interactively related to student outcomes of attrition or performance.

Interaction effects between grading practice and work-pace variables were analyzed with all of the variables entered. No interaction effects were identified when *grading practice–work-pace* was added to the equation. The interaction for the combined variables of *sex, ability, grading practice, and work-pace for student performance* was not significant.

Appendix D1

Example of a Face-to-Face Paper Rubric

In the comparison of student outcomes across face-to-face, flip-hybrid, and online courses, the requirements of the courses were reviewed. Requirements across the courses included student writing assignments. An example of one of the rubics (of the three required papers for the face-to-face and hybrid courses) is titled: Attachment, Temperament, Cognitive Development, Psychosocial Development, Longevity for 31 points of 300 points. Each of three papers equivalent to 10 percent of course grade.

Part 1: Read the information in your text regarding attachment styles and find and complete an online inventory on attachment styles. Summarize the theory and your perceptions of the theory. You do not have to describe your own attachment score. But do explain the meanings of the differing scores in terms of early experience and later personal relationships.

Part 2: Find and complete an online survey of Temperament. You do not have to divulge your score. What you need to do is describe the kinds of temperament and relate how an individual's temperament can affect attachment, psychosocial stage development, and cognitive development.

Part 3: Describe your own experiences or someone you know well in terms of each of the first four stages of Piaget's Theory of Cognitive Development. Make sure to include a hallmark of each stage and why you believe each incident is a good descriptor of the given stage.

Part 1, 2, and 3: Due by stated date, midnight in SafeAssign (link at bottom of Assignment Page) for 15 pts. (Word count for this portion should be between 1,200 and 1,500 words, including the references. Reference your text and the online assessments, plus any other sources. You will not lose points regarding formatting (such as APA or MLA) because much of this is not maintained in the SafeAssign submission. You will lose points for multiple spelling errors.

Part 4: Review Erikson's psychosocial stages in your text and view the mini-lecture: http://education-portal.com/academy/lesson/eriksons-stages-of-identity-formation. (You can copy and paste the URL into your browser.) Write a (minimum 5-sentence) paragraph on the first 7 of the 8 stages. In your paragraph describe the psychosocial development of yourself or someone you know well. For each stage, do you think the person you are describing completed the stage with a positive or a negative outcome? Explain your reasoning.

Part 5: Find and complete a Longevity (how long will you live) Survey. Summarize the meaning of your score related to your current lifestyle/life choices. Here are two choices:

Part 4 and 5: Due date, by midnight in SafeAssign link at bottom of Assignment Page for 16 pts. At the bottom of your paper you must reference your textbook, each of the surveys and video clips you utilized (including URLs), and other sources. The word count should be between 1,200 and 1,500 words, including the references, as noted above. Submit paper to SafeAssign link in the course website. Points will be deducted for poor citing/plagiarism.

Appendix D2

Online Essay and
Essay Response Rubrics

Essay Rubric (12 pts.) To earn full credit essay must:

1. Essays are due by 3 p.m. on Thursday each week in course discussion board (copy & pasted) and SafeAssign (as an attachment through links in Bb WEEKLY folders). Late essays earn reduced credit. After 3 weeks, late essays no longer graded. (Complete essays in advance, then you can earn full credit, WHEN a problem occurs.)
2. SafeAssign (SA) scores above 25 with long passages copied (even w/cite) may have points deducted (w/out concurrent higher word count). SA is an anti-plagiarism program that color codes all sentences and paragraphs of your essays showing sources. Points are deducted when a student submits another's work, without referencing. Points are not submitted to GradeBook for essays without the SA report. Review your SA report each week to improve your academic writing.
3. Support your essay with evidence (research/credible sources) from text/other sources. Four sources, including text, lecture video, and assigned articles/video clips required per essay. (-1 pt.) for each missing reference and (-½ pt.) for incomplete reference, include URL and title minimum, for each video clip source.
4. Relate the question in some way to your own experience, something you have read, or film you have viewed (-1–3 pts.) if essay does not include relevance to your life.
5. Each essay must address the assigned videos, notes, and survey. Each video clip and survey summary are worth 2–3 pts. (-1 pt. each) for lacking URL + title minimum for video and title + author minimum for survey.

6. Answer the discussion board questions with a minimum of 600 words in length, including video clip/s and survey summary (–½ pt. per each 30 words short). Post your word total below your references. The Essay questions/topics and the essay references are NOT counted in the word count.

ESSAY RESPONSE RUBRIC

(3 pts. + 2 extra credit points possible for additional peer feedback)

1. Read, then kindly and respectfully comment on a minimum of one essay (0 points if not kind and respectful). The essay response is due by 3 p.m. Friday, of each week.
2. If the essay response is lacking length/other requirements (such as pointing out where the essay responding to does not meet the essay rubric: length, references, discussing the videos) –½ credit. Addressing these issues allows the essayist to correct and earn the full points on the essay. (Corrections are monitored in discussion board).
3. "I agree with you" or "Keep up the good work" is inadequate. Explain your reasoning and evidence for agreement/disagreement. Your response must be "value added" (i.e., What are you bringing to the discussion?). Full credit essay response must be a minimum of 150 words with word count included. A longer essay response or an additional essay response can add up to an additional 2 pts. of extra credit. Essay responses submitted Sunday evening after the due date are not graded.

Appendix D3

Course Design and Student Outcome Statistical Discussion and Tables

None of the three instructional groups had a normal distribution. The significant Levene's test confirmed the lack of homogeneity of variance, a violation of an assumption required to conduct parametric statistical analyses. High correlations of some grades across the three course designs indicate that multicollinearity is also an issue within the data (Morgan, Leech, Gloeckner, & Barrett, 2007). The independent variable of this study, Instructional Design, consists of three independent nominal groups. The dependent variable, "Grades," is ordinal with four levels: 1) As, 2) Bs, 3) Cs, and 4) D, or F, or W.

A one-way analysis of variance (ANOVA) was conducted to determine differences in student outcomes across the groups. ANOVA analyses are robust to violations of normality when assumptions are markedly violated. A Kruskal-Wallis test for independent K samples is recommended for nonparametric, ordinal data when equal variances cannot be justified (Morgan et al., 2007).

Both of these analyses were conducted, with statistically significant differences found between the three instructional groups for the four levels of grades (when entered all together as ordinal grades): $F_{(2,384)} = 17.42$, $(p < .000)$. When grades were entered as dichotomous (i.e., DFW or not DFW), the following differences were noted; DFW: $F_{(2,384)} = 16.42$, $(p < .001)$; C– to C+: $F_{(2,384)} = 5.43$, $(p = .005)$; B– to B+: $F_{(2,384)} = 2.63$, $(p = .073)$; A– to A: $F_{(2,384)} = 11.67$, $(p < .001)$.

Results for the conservative Kruskal-Wallis analysis $(p < .001)$ corroborated significant differences found in the ANOVA between grade outcomes across the three instructional groups, stating that the null hypothesis of no difference was rejected. A table showing the Kruskal-Wallis test for significance with nominal and ordinal data is presented in table D3.1.

Table D3.1. Independent Samples Kruskal-Wallis Test Summary Comparing Student Outcomes for Face-to-Face, Flip-Hybrid, and Online Course Instructional Designs

	Null hypothesis	*Sig.*	*Decision*
1	`	.000	Reject the null hypothesis
2	The distribution of Cs is the same across courses.	.005	Reject the null hypothesis
3	The distribution of Bs is the same across courses.	.073	Retain the null hypothesis
4	The distribution of As is the same across courses.	.000	Reject the null hypothesis

Asymptotic significances displayed; $p = 05$.

Due to the significant findings of the ANOVA and Kruskal-Wallis test, an overall ANOVA was conducted without B grades, as these were not significantly different across groups as reported in the ANOVA for all of the data. The following differences were reported (for all except Bs): $F_{(2,290)} = 18.22$, $(p < .001)$.

Table D3.2 reports the following significant results for each grade difference (without the Bs entered into the equation) by instructional design. The A grades across the three course designs were the only value that did not have a significant Levene's test indicating that the assumption of homogeneity of variances had not been violated.

Table D3.2. One-Way Analysis of Variance Summary Table Comparing Student Performance Outcomes for Three Instructional Course Designs

Student Outcome	*Instructional Groups*	*SS*	*MS*	*F*
	Between groups	16.17	8.09	10.98
D, F, or W	Within groups	212.20	.74	
	Total	228.37	68	
	Between groups	21.05	10.53	7.25
C grades	Within groups	418.06	1.45	
	Total	439.11		
	Between groups	241.36	120.68	22.66
A grades	Within groups	1,533.89	5.32	
	Total	1,775.26		

df (2, 290); $p < .001$.

The student outcomes of three instructional course designs were analyzed using analysis of variance (ANOVA) and checked with the Kruskal-Wallis tests, for non-parametric (not bell-shaped) data. Due to the significant findings of the ANOVA and Kruskal-Wallis test, a post hoc was completed using the Games-Howell statistic recommended for unequal variances, such as with the three instructional groups in this study. The significant post hoc results for the three instructional designs and the DFW, Cs, and As are reported in table D3.3.

Table D3.3.   Games-Howell Post Hoc for Student Outcome Differences for Instructional Designs

Student Outcome	Instructional Groups	N	MD	SE
D, F, or W	Face-to-face by flip-hybrid	45	−.57	.12
	Face-to-face by online	54	−.43	.11
C grades	Flip-hybrid by online	45	.65	.18
A grades	Face-to-face by flip-hybrid	90	2.03	.34
	Face-to-face by online	112	1.91	.33

$p < .001$; face-to face $n = 91$, flip-hybrid $n = 94$, online $n = 106$

Table D3.3 shows that there were significant differences between instructional groups compared for specific student outcomes, not for all of the student outcomes included in the analyses. Because the assumptions of normal distributions for the dependent variable of student grades and the homogeneity of variances were violated, the results should be viewed with caution.

Games-Howell post hoc tests revealed that student outcomes were statistically different for *face-to-face* compared with *flip-hybrid* courses for *DFWs* and *As*; that *face-to-face* compared with *online* courses were also significantly different for *DFWs* and *As*; and that *flip-hybrid* compared with *online* courses were significantly different for student outcomes of *Cs*. For all *DFWs* ($d = .07$) *Cs* ($d = .05$) *As* ($d = .14$).

Effect sizes (reported as *d's* for ANOVA) were determined by dividing the Between Groups Sum of Squares by the Total Sum of Squares reported in the ANOVA analysis ($p = < .001$). These effect sizes are all medium to large according to the literature.

References

Abdul-Alim, J. (2015). Diversity in the virtual classroom. *Insight into Diversity, 86*(3). http://www.insightintodiversity.com/wp-content/media/issues/december2015.pdf.

Adelman, C. (1999). *Answers in the tool box: Intensity, attendance patterns, and bachelor's degree attainment.* Washington, DC: Office of Educational Research and Improvement, U.S. Department of Education.

Adelman, C. (2004). *The empirical curriculum: Changes in postsecondary course-taking, 1972–2000.* Washington, DC: Office of Educational Research and Improvement, U.S. Department of Education.

American Academy of Arts and Sciences. (2016). *Public Research Universities: Serving the Public Good.* Cambridge, MA: The Lincoln Project. https://www.amacad.org/content.aspx?d=22174.

American Academy of Arts & Sciences (2017). *The Future of undergraduate education: The Future of America.* Cambridge MA: The Commission on the Future of Undergraduate Education.

American Association for Higher Education. (2006). *Assessment forum.* Accessed from the website: http://www.aahe.org/assessment/ on 06/07/06.

American Association of Community Colleges (AACC). (2016, September). Time to degree: A national view of the time enrolled and elapsed for associate and bachelor's degree earners. Research Center. https://www.nscresearchcenter.org/signaturereport11/.

American Association of Higher Education (AAHE). (2005). Principles of good practice for assessing student learning. http://www.teaching.uncc.edu/best-practice/education-philosophy/assessing-student-learning.

American Association of Higher Education (AAHE). (2006). Assessment Forum. http://www.aahe.org/assessment/.

American Educational Research Association (AERA). (2011, February). AERA code of ethics and ethical standards of the American Educational Research Association: Cases and commentary. http://www.aera. net/Portals/38/docs/About_AERA/CodeOfEthics.

American Psychological Association. (2015). *National guidelines and suggested learning outcomes for the undergraduate psychology major* (draft 10). http://www.Apa.org/ed/draft10 .html/ (accessed 4/18/16).

Arthur, W., Tubre, T., Paul, D., & Edens, P. (2003). Teaching effectiveness: The relationship between reaction and learning evaluation criteria. *Educational Psychology: An International Journal of Experimental Educational Psychology, 23*(3), 275–285.

Arum, R., Roksa, J., & Cook, A. (2016). *Improving quality in American higher education: Learning outcomes and assessments for the 21st century.* San Francisco: Jossey-Bass.

Astin, A., & Oseguera, L. (2002). *Degree attainment rates at American colleges and universities.* Los Angeles: University of California, Higher Educational Research Institute.

Atherton, M. (2014, November). Academic Preparedness of First-Generation College Students: Different Perspectives. *Journal of College Student Development. 55*(8): 824–829.

Aultman, L. (2006). An unexpected benefit of formative student evaluations. *College Teaching, 54*(3), 251.

Babcock, P., & Marks, M. (2011). The Falling Time Cost of College: Evidence from Half a Century of Time Use Data. *The Review of Economics and Statistics 93*(2) 468–478.

Bailey, T., Jaggars, S., & Scott-Clayton, J. (2013, Spring). Characterizing the Effectiveness of Developmental Education: A Response to Recent Criticism. *Journal of Developmental Education 36*(3): 18–22.

Bain, K. (2004). *What the best college teachers do.* Cambridge, MA: Harvard University Press.

Bambara, C., Harbour, C., Davies, T. G., & Athey, S. (2009). Delicate engagement: The lived experience of community college students enrolled in high-risk online courses. *Community College Review, 36*(3), 219–238.

Banta, T., Jones, E., & Black, K. (2009). *Designing effective assessment: Principles and profiles of good practice.* San Francisco: Jossey-Bass.

Banta, T. (Ed.). (2004). *Community college assessment.* San Francisco: Jossey-Bass.

Banta, T., Black, K., Kahn, S., & Jackson, J. (2004, Summer). A perspective on good practice in community college assessment. *New Directions for Community Colleges, 126,* 5–16.

Barak, R., & Kniker, C. (2002, Summer). Benchmarking by state higher education boards. *New Directions for Higher Education, 118,* 93–102.

Barefoot, B., & Gardner, N. (Ed.). (2005). *Achieving and sustaining institutional excellence for the first year of college.* San Francisco: Jossey-Bass.

Barshay, J. (2015, May). The online paradox at community colleges. Education by the numbers. *The Hechenger Report.* http://www.hechingerreport.org/the-online-paradox-at -community-colleges/.

Benjamin, T. (2015, Fall). Indicators of socio-economic status. Ohio Association Institute of Research and Planning (OAIRP). http://www.oairp.org/Indicators_of_Socioeconomic_ Status(SES).pdf.

Beran, T., & Violato, C. (2005, December). Ratings of university teacher instruction: How much do student and course characteristics really matter? *Assessment and Evaluation in Higher Education, 30*(6), 593–601.

Berliner, D., & Glass, G. (Eds.). (2014). *50 Myths and Lies That Threaten America's Public Schools: The Real Crisis in Education.* New York: Teachers College, Columbia University.

Berrett, D. (2014, February & August). How 'flipping' the classroom can improve the traditional lecture. *The Chronicle of Higher Education.*

Bers, T., & Calhoun, H. (2004, Spring). Literature on community colleges: An overview. *New Directions for Community Colleges, 117,* 5–12.

Bishop, T., & Verlager, M. (2013, July). *The flipped classroom: A survey of the research.* 120th ASEE Annual Conference & Exposition, Atlanta. Paper I.D. # 6219.

Bjork, R., Dunlosky, J., & Kornell, N. (2013). Self-regulated learning: Beliefs, techniques, and illusions. *Annual Review of Psychology, 64,* 417–444. https://www.doi.org/10.1146/annurev-psych-113011-143823.

Blaich, B., Wise, K., Pascarella, E., & Roksa, J. (2016). Instructional Clarity and Organization: It's Not New or Fancy, But It Matters. *Change: The Magazine of Higher Learning 48*(4): 6–13.

Bloom, B., Hastings, J., & Madaus, G. (1991). *Handbook on formative and summative evaluation of student learning.* New York: McGraw-Hill.

Boettcher, J., & Conrad, R. (2010). *The online teaching survival guide: Simple and practical pedagogical tips* (1st ed.). San Francisco: Jossey Bass. https://www.innovateonline.info/index.php?view=article&id=54.

Boggs, G. (2001, Winter). Community colleges at a crossroads. *Presidency, 4*(1) 14–21. (ERIC # EJ625076, retrieved 06/12/2006).

Bonesronning, H. (August, 2004). Do the teacher's grading practices affect student achievement? *Education Economics, 12*(2).

Borden, V., & Owens, J. (2001). *Measuring quality: Choosing among surveys and other assessments of college quality.* Washington, DC: American Council on Education.

Bordens, K., & Abbott, B. (2004). *Research design and methods: A process approach* (6th ed.). Boston: McGraw-Hill.

Boretz, E. (2004, Spring). Grade inflation and the myth of student consumerism. *College Teaching, 52*(2), 42.

Boysen, G. (2016). Using student evaluations to improve teaching: Evidence-based recommendations. *Scholarship of Teaching and Learning, 2,* 273–284.

Bracey, G. (2006). *Reading educational research: How to avoid getting statistically snookered.* Portsmouth, NH: Heinemann.

Braxton, J., Hirschy, A., & McClendon, S. (2004). Understanding and reducing college student departure. *ASHE Higher Education Report, 30*(3).

Brookhart, S. (2004, December). Assessment theory for college classrooms. *New Directions for Teaching & Learning, 100,* 5–14.

Brookhart, S. (2015). Graded achievement, tested achievement, and validity. *Educational Assessment 20*(4): 268–296.

Browers, A., & Tomic, W. (2001, June). The factorial validity of scores on the teacher interpersonal self-efficacy scale. *Educational and Psychological Measurement, 61*(3), 433–445.

Burke, J. (Ed.). (2006). *Achieving accountability in higher education: Balancing public, academic, and market demands.* San Francisco: Jossey-Bass.

Butler, S., & McMunn, N. (2006). *A teacher's guide to classroom assessment: Understanding and using assessment to improve student learning.* San Francisco: Jossey-Bass.

Canning, E., & Harackiewicz, J. (2015). Teach it, don't preach it: The differential effects of directly-communicated and self-generated utility–value information. *Motivation Science, 1*(1), 47.

Cassidy, S. (2011). Self-regulated learning in higher education: identifying key component processes. *Studies in Higher Education 36*(8): 989–1000.

Centra, J. (2003, October). Will teachers receive higher student evaluations by giving higher grades and less course work? *Research in Higher Education, 44*(5), 495–518.

Chetty, R., Friedman, J., Saez, E., Turner, N., & Yagan, D. (2017, July). *Mobility Report Cards: The Role of Colleges in Intergenerational Mobility*. http:// www.equality-of-opportunity.org/papers/coll_mrc_paper.pdf.

Clark, L., & Smouse, C. (2017). You need this list of 17 best course practices. Higher Education Blackboard Innovative Teaching Strategies Blackboard Innovative Teaching Strategies (BITS). https://help.blackboard.com/Learn/Instructor/Performance/Best_Practices/Online_Teaching_Strategies/BITS_2017.

Coe, R. (2002, September). *It's the effect size, stupid. What effect size is and why it is important.* University of Exeter, England, 12-14: Paper presented at the Annual Conference of the British Educational Research Association. http://www.leeds.ac.uk/educol/documents/00002182.htm.

Cohen, J. (1988). *Statistical power and analysis for the behavioral sciences* (2nd ed.). Hillsdale, NJ: Lawrence Erlbaum Associates.

Cohen, J. (1994). The earth is round (p < .05). *American Psychologist, 49*, 997–1003.

College Board. (2014). *Trends in Student Aid.* https://secure-media.collegeboard.org/digitalServices/misc/trends/2014-trends-student-aid-report-final.pdf.

Community College Research Center (CCRC). (2015, April). What we know about online course outcomes. Teachers College, Columbia University. http://www.ccrrc.tc.columbia.edu.

Community College Survey of Student Engagement (CCSSE). (2017). Center for Community College Student Engagement, a research and service initiative program in higher education leadership, Department of Educational Administration, College of Education, The University of Texas at Austin. http://www.ccsse. org/aboutsurvey/aboutsurvey.cfm.

Culatta, R., & Speicher, S. (2016, October). Shadow those students, for their own good. *Chronicle of Higher Education*, p. B25.

Darling-Hammond, L. (2000, January). Teacher quality and student achievement: A review of state policy evidence. *Education Policy Analysis Archives, 8*(1).

Darling-Hammond, L. (2016, March). Research on Teaching and Teacher Education and Its Influences on Policy and Practice. *Educational Researcher 45*(2): 83–91.

Davis, T., & Hillman Murrell, P. (1994). Turning teaching into learning: The role of student responsibility in the collegiate experience. *ASHE-ERIC Higher Education Reports*, Report 8. Washington, DC: The George Washington University. (ERIC# 372702, accessed 7/15/06).

Deming, D., & Dynarski, S. (2010). *Into College, Out of Poverty? Policies to Increase the Postsecondary Attainment of the Poor*, 283–302. University of Chicago Press.

DeNavas-Walt, C., & Proctor, B. (2014). *U.S. Census Bureau*, Current Population Reports, P60-252, Income and Poverty in the United States: U.S. Government Printing Office, Washington, DC.

Doherty, R. W., Hilberg, S., & Epaloose, G. (2002, November/December). Standards performance continuum: Development and validation of a measure of effective pedagogy. *Journal of Educational Research, 96*, 78–102.

Driscoll, M. (2015). *Psychology for Learning and Instruction*. Needham Heights, MA: Allyn & Bacon.

Dumford, A., Cogswell, C., & Miller, A. (2016). The who, what, and where of learning strategies. *The Journal of Effective Teaching, 16*(1).

Dunlosky, J., Rawson, K., Marsh, E., Nathan, M., & Willingham, D. (2013). Improving students' learning with effective learning techniques: promising directions from cognitive and educational psychology. *Psychological Science in the Public Interest 14*(1): 4–58.

Dunn, D., Mehrotra, C., & Halonen, J. (2004). *Measuring up: Educational assessment challenges and practices for psychology*. Washington, DC, American Psychological Association.

Dweck, C. (2016). *Mindset: The new psychology of success.* New York: Random House.

Eagan, K., & Jaeger, A. (2009, March). Effects of exposure to part-time faculty on community college transfer. *Research in Higher Education, 50*(2), 168–188.

Ellis, M. (2013). Successful community college transfer students speak out. *Community College Journal of Research and Practice 37*(2).

Elton, L. (2004). Goodhart's law and performance indicators in higher education. *Evaluation and Research in Education, 18*(1).

Fang, M. (2013, August 2). Nearly 80 percent of students work while in school. *Think Progress.* https://www.thinkprogress.org/nearly-80-percent-of-students-work-while-in-school-2f44edacd275.

Fast Facts (2013–2014). School student population report. Mid-sized midwestern community college. http:www.muskgoncc.edu.

Fear, F., Doberneck, D., Robinson, C., Fear, K., Barr, R., Van Den Berg, H., Smith, J., & Petrulis, R. (2003). The learning paradigm: A provocative idea in practice. *Innovative Higher Education, 27*(3), 151–168. (ERIC # EJ666470, retrieved: 05/06/06).

Fink, D. (2013). *Creating Significant Experiences Revised and Updated: An Integrated Approach to Designing College Courses.* San Francisco: John Wiley & Sons.

Firat, M., & Yuzer, T. (2016). Learning analytics: assessment of mass data in distance education." *International Journal on New Trends in Education and their Implications 7*(2). www.ijonte.org/FileUpload/ks63207/File/01.mehmet_firat_.pdf.

Fossey, R., & Wood, R. (2004, Spring). Academic freedom and tenure. *New Directions for Community Colleges, 125,* 51–63. (Retrieved 2/27/06).

Fraenkel, J., & Wallen, N. (2006). *How to design and evaluate research in education* (3rd ed.). New York: McGraw-Hill.

Freedman, J. (2016, November). On changing minds. *Chronicle of Higher Education,* p. B8.

Friedlander, J., & Serban, A. (2004, Summer). Meeting the challenges of assessing student learning outcomes. *New Directions for Community Colleges, 126,* 101–109.

Fuchs, L., & Fuchs, D. (1996, November). Effects of systematic formative evaluation: A meta-analysis. *Exceptional Children, 53*(3), 199–208.

Gabriel, K. (2008). *Teaching unprepared students: Strategies for promoting success and retention in higher education.* Sterling, VA: Stylus Publishing.

Gawande, A. (2016, June). The mistrust of science. *The New Yorker.* https://www.farnam-streetblog.com/2016/06/atul-gawande-mistrust-science/.

Gladwell, M. (2011). *Outliers: The story of success.* New York: Little Brown and Company.

Gliner, J., & Morgan, G. (2000). *Research in applied settings: An integrated approach.* Mahwah, NJ: Erlbaum.

Graesser, A. (2011). Learning, thinking, and emoting with discourse technologies. *American Psychologist, 66,* 743–757.

Greenwald, A., & Gillmore, G. (1997). No pain, no gain? The importance of measuring course workload in student ratings of instruction. *Journal of Educational Psychology, 89*(4).

Grubb, N. (1999). *Honored but invisible: An inside look at teaching in community colleges.* New York: Routledge Press.

Guskey, T. (Ed.) (2009). *Practical Solutions for Serious Problems in Standards-Based Grading.* Thousand Oaks, CA: Corwin Press.

Guskey, T. (2013). Defining student achievement. In J. Hattie & E. Anderman (Eds.). *Handbook of Student Achievement,* 3–6. NY: Routledge.

Habanek, D. (2005). An examination of the integrity of the syllabus. *College Teaching, 53,* 62–64.

Habley, W., Bloom, J., & Robbins, S. (2012). *Increasing persistence: Research-based strategies for college student success.* Hoboken, NJ: John Wiley & Sons Inc.

Haertel, E. (2013). *Reliability and validity of inferences about teachers based on student test scores.* Princeton, NJ: Educational Testing Service.

Halpern, D. (1993). Targeting outcomes: Covering your assessment needs. In T. McGovern, ed., *Handbook for enhancing undergraduate education in psychology.* Washington, DC: American Psychological Association, 23–70.

Halpern, D., & Hakel, M. (2003, July/August). Applying the science of learning to the university and beyond: Teaching for long-term retention and transfer. *Change, 35*(4), 36–41.

Hamilton, N. (2002). *Academic ethics: Problems and materials on professional conduct and shared governance.* American Council on Education. New York: Greenwood Publishing Group.

Hanushek, E., & Rivkin, S. (2010, May). Generalizations about using value-added measures of teacher quality. *American Economic Review, 2*(100), 267–271.

Hargreaves, A., Earl, L., & Schmidt, M. (2002, Spring). Alternative assessment reform. *American Educational Research Journal, 39*(1).

Harrison, P., Ryan, J., & Moore, P. (1996, December). College students' self-insight and common implicit theories in ratings of teaching effectiveness. *Journal of Educational Psychology, 88*(4), 775–782.

Hartlep, K., & Forsyth, G. (2000). The effect of self-reference on learning and retention. *Teaching of Psychology, 27*(4).

Hattie, J. (2011). *Visible learning for teachers: Maximizing impact on learning* (1st ed.). New York: Routledge.

Heckert, T., Latier, A., Ringwald, A., & Silvey, B. (2006). Correlations of teaching evaluation dimensions with each other and with course, instructor and student characteristics. *College Student Journal, 40*(1).

Higher Education Report. (2004). Beyond grade inflation. ASHE-ERIC *Higher Education Report, 30*(6). (ERIC # 17113788. Retrieved March, 2006).

Higher Learning Commission (HLC). (2001). *Addendum to the handbook of accreditation* (2nd ed.). Chicago: Author.

Hinton, C., Fischer, K., & Glennon, C. (2012). Mind, brain and education. In *Jobs for the Future; Students at the Center: Teaching and Learning in the Era of the Common Core.* Boston: JFF.

Honeycutt, B., Garrett, J., & Glova, S. (2014, July). Expanding the definition of a flipped learning environment. In Mary Bart (Ed.), *Faculty Focus Special Report: Blended and flipped: Exploring new models for effective teaching.* Magna Publication. http//www.FacultyFocus.com.

Hornby, W. (2003). Assessing using grade-related criteria: A single currency for universities? *Assessment & Evaluation in Higher Education, 28*(4).

Hu, H., & Driscoll, M. (2013, October). Self-regulation in e-learning environments: A remedy for community college? *Journal of Educational Technology & Society, 16*(4), 171–184.

Hulleman, C., & Barron, K. (2016). Motivation Interventions in Education: Bridging Theory, Research, and Practice. In Corno, L. & Anderman, E. (Eds.). (2016). *Handbook of Educational Psychology*, 3rd ed. NY: Routledge.

Isely, P., & Singh, H. (2005, Winter). Do higher grades lead to favorable student evaluations? *Journal of Economic Education, 36*(1).

Johnson, A. (2003). *What every teacher should know about action research.* Boston: Pearson Educational Inc.

Johnston, G., & Kristovich, S. (2000, Spring). Community college alchemists: Turning data into information. *New Directions for Community Colleges, 109*, 63–74.

Jones, V., & Jones, L. (2001). *Comprehensive classroom management: Creating communities of support and solving problems* (6th ed.). Boston: Allyn & Bacon.

Juszkiewicz, J. (2016, March). *Trends in community college enrollment and completion data,* 2016, Washington, DC: American Association of Community Colleges.

Kaplin, W., & Lee, B. (2006). *The law of higher education: A comprehensive guide to legal implications of administrative decision making* (6th ed.). San Francisco: Jossey-Bass.

Katzer, J., Cook, K., & Crouch W. (1991). *Evaluating information: A guide for users of social science research* (3rd ed.). New York: McGraw-Hill, Inc.

Keith, K., Hammer, E., Blair-Broeker, C., & Ernst, R. (2013). High school psychology: A coming of age story. *Teaching of Psychology, 40*(4), 311–317.

Kember, D. (2004). Interpreting student workload and the factors which shape students' perceptions of their workload. *Studies in Higher Education, 29*(2), 165–184.

Keup, J. (2004, March–April). Cooperative Institutional Research Program (CIRP) Freshman Survey and Your First College Year: Using Longitudinal Data to Assess the First Year of College. *Assessment Update 16*(2): 8–10.

Kezar, A., & Maxey, D. (2014, Fall). Faculty Matter: So Why Doesn't Everyone Think So? *Thought and Action,* 29–44.

Kihlstrom, J. (2016). How students learn: A perspective from cognitive and social psychology. GSI Center How Students Learn Project. http://gsi.berkeley.edu/programs-services/hsl-project/hsl-speakers/kihlstrom/.

Kilgo, C., Ezell Sheets, J. & Pascarella, E. (2015).The Link between High-Impact Practices and Student Learning: Some Longitudinal Evidence. *Higher Education: The International Journal of Higher Education and Educational Planning 69*(4): 509–525.

Kinzie, J., Cogswell, C., & Wheatle, K. (2015). Reflections on the state of student engagement data use and strategies for action. *Assessment Update, 27*(2).

Kiziliak, R., Saltarelli, A., Reich, J., & Cohen, G. (2017, January). Closing global achievement gaps in MOOCs. *Science 355*(6322): 251–225. http://science.sciencemag.org/content/355/6322/251.

Kuh, G. (2003). What we're learning about student engagement from NSSE. *Change, 35*(2), 24–32.

Kuh, G., Kinzie, J., Shuh, J., & Whitt, E. (2006). *Assessing conditions to enhance educational effectiveness: The inventory for student engagement and success.* San Francisco: Jossey-Bass.

Kurtzleben, D. (2014, February 11). Study: Income gap between young college and high school grads widens. *US News.* (Accessed 2017, March). https://www.usnews.com/news/articles/2014/02/11/study-income-gap-between-young-college-and-high-school-grads-widens.

Landrum, E., & Gurung, R. (2013). The memorability of introductory psychology revisited. *Teaching of Psychology, 40*(3), 222–227.

Le, C., & Wolfe, R. (2013). How can schools boost students' self-regulation? Teaching students how to take responsibility for their own effort can enable them to become more persistent and focused about learning. *Phi Delta Kappan, 95*(2), 33.

Leathwood, C. (2005, June). Assessment policy and practice in higher education: Purpose, standards and equity. *Assessment & Evaluation in Higher Education, 30*(3).

Lewis, C. (2015, July). Academic freedom and intellectual integrity. *Filed Under: Sexual Harassment Project.* http://www.cynthialewis.net/category/sexual-harassment-project/.

Looney, A. (2017). A Comparison between the College Scorecard and Mobility Report Cards. https://www.treasury.gov/connect/blog/Pages/ A-Comparison-between-the-College-Scorecard-and-Mobility-Report-Cards.aspx.

Lundenburg, F., & Ornstein, A. (2004). *Educational administration: Concepts and practices.* Boston: Cengage Learning.

Marsh, H. (2007). Students evaluation of university teaching dimensionality, reliability, validity, potential biases and usefulness. In R. Perry and J. Smart (Eds.). *The Scholarship of Teaching and Learning in Higher Education: An Evidence-Based Perspective,* 319–383. Springer.

Marsh, H., & Roche, L. (2000, March). Effects of grading leniency and low workload on students' evaluations of teaching: Popular myth, bias, validity, or innocent bystanders? *Journal of Educational Psychology, 92*(1), 202–208.

Marzano, R., Pickering, D., & Pollack, J. (2001). *Classroom instruction that works: Research based strategies for increasing student achievement.* Alexandria, VA: McRel Institute.

Marzano, R. (2003). *What works in schools: Translating research into action.* Alexandria, VA: Association for Supervision and Curriculum Development.

Marzano, R. (2007). *The art and science of teaching: A comprehensive framework for effective instruction.* Alexandria, VA: Association for Supervision and Curriculum Development.

Massy, W. (2016). *Reengineering the University: How to be Mission Centered, Market Smart, and Margin Conscious.* Baltimore: Johns Hopkins University Press.

McKeachie, W. (2002). *McKeachie's teaching tips: Strategies, research, and theory for college and university teachers* (11th ed.). New York: Houghton Mifflin.

McPhail, C., & McPhail, I. (2006). Prioritizing community college missions: A directional effort. *New Directions for Community Colleges, 136,* 91–99.

Merriam, S., & Cafferella, R. (Eds.). (1999). *Learning in adulthood.* San Francisco: Jossey-Bass.

Midwestern College Handbook and *Midwestern Community College Impact Statement.* (2010). X, MI: X Community College.

Morgan, G., Gliner, J., & Harmon, R. (2001). *Understanding research methods and statistics: A practitioner's guide for evaluating research.* Mahwah, NJ: Lawrence Erlbaum Associates Publishers.

Morgan, G., Leech, N., Gloeckner, G., & Barrett, K. (2007). *IBM SPSS for intermediate statistics: Use and interpretation* (5th ed.). New York: Routledge Publishers.

Morris, L. (2004, Winter). Exploring the learning paradigm. *Innovative Higher Education, 29*(2).

Moxley, D., Dubrigue, C., & Najor-Durack, A. (2001). *Keeping students in higher education: Successful strategies and practices for retention.* London: Kogan.

Nasser, R., & McInerney, D. (2016). Achievement-oriented beliefs and their relation to academic expectations and school achievement. *Educational Psychology: An International Journal of Experimental Educational Psychology, 36*(7), 1219–1241.

National Center for Educational Statistics (NCES). (2007). College Board Annual Survey of Colleges, Online Nation: Five years of growth in online learning. http://www.nces.ed.gov/ipeds/.

National Center for Educational Statistics (NCES). (2015a). College Board Annual Survey of Colleges, The Condition of Education, 2015. http://www.nces.ed.gov/ipeds/.

National Center for Educational Statistics (NCES). (2015b). Demographic and Enrollment Characteristics of Nontraditional Undergraduates. https://nces.ed.gov/pubs 2015/2015025.pdf.

National Research Council. (2001). *Knowing what students know: The science and design of educational assessment.* Washington, DC: National Academy Press.

National Research Council. (2008). *Assessing accomplished teaching: Advanced-level certification programs.* Washington, DC: The National Academies Press.

National Student Clearinghouse (NSC). (2013–2016). What are the different types of student pathways? http://www.studentclearinghouse.org/colleges/studenttracker/.

National Survey of Student Engagement (NCCE) (2003). The College Student Report Overview. http://nsse.indiana.edu/pdf/2003_inst_report/NSSE_2003_Overview.pdf.

Neshyba, S. (2014, April). It's a flipping revolution. A guide to the flipped classroom. *The Chronicle of Higher Education.*

Nilson, L. (2013). *Creating self-regulated learners: Strategies to strengthen students' self-awareness and learning skills.* Sterling, VA: Stylus Publishing.

Noel-Levitz, R. (2012). Student retention and college completion. White papers, trend reports, and other resources *National Freshman Motivation to Complete College Reports.* https://www.ruffalonl.com/papers-research-higher-education-fundraising/student-retention-white-papers-and-trend-reports.

Norusis, M. (2015). *SPSS 12. 0 Statistical procedures.* Upper Saddle River, NJ: Prentice Hall.

O'Banion, T. (2012). Late registration: May it rest in peace. *Community College Journal, 83*(1), 26–31. Retrieved from ERIC database. (EJ999546).

O'Banion, T. (2016, July). Helping students make a good living and live a good life: Colleges must bridge the divide between technical and liberal education. *Community College Week.*

O'Connor, K. (2017). *How to Grade for Learning: Linking Grades to Standards.* Thousand Oaks, CA: Corwin Press.

Ohmann, R. (2000). Historical reflections on accountability. *Academe* (retrieved from http://www.aaup.org/publications, 7/21/04).

Ormrod, J. (2006). *Essentials of educational psychology.* Upper Saddle River, NJ: Merrill Prentice Hall.

Orozco, V., & Cauthen, N. (2009). Work less, study more & succeed. Demos: A network for ideas & action. *Postsecondary Success Series.* http://www.demos.org/sites/default.files/publications/WorkLessStudyMore_Demos.pdf.

O'Shea, D. (June, 2017). What's Wrong with Too Many Required Courses? Inside Higher Education. https://www.insidehighered.com/views/2017/06/27/unintended-consequences-too-many-requirements-essay.

Pallas, A., Neumann, A., & Campbell, C. (2017). *Policies and Practices to Support Undergraduate Teaching Improvement.* Cambridge, MA: American Academy of Arts and Sciences.

Pascarella, W., Seifert, T., & Whitt, E. (2008, Fall). Effective instruction and college student persistence: Some new evidence. *New Directions for Teaching and Learning, 2008*(115), 55–70.

Pellegrino, J. W., & Hilton, M. L. (Eds.). (2012). *Education for life and work: Developing transferable knowledge and skills in the 21st century.* Washington, DC: National Academies Press.

Perna, L., (Ed.). (2010, August-July). *New research shows that students are working more and juggling a multitude of roles, creating anxiety and lowering graduation rates.* AAUP Report. Sterling, VA: Stylus.

Perry, R. (2004, December). Intimations of the 21st century. *Educational Research and Evaluation, 10*(4-6), 551–558.

Popham, W. (2005). *Classroom assessment: What teachers need to know* (4th ed.). Boston: Allyn & Bacon Publishers.

Pruett, P. & Absher, B. (2015, Summer). Factors Influencing Retention of Developmental Education Students in Community Colleges. *Delta Kappa Gamma Bulletin 81*(4): 32–40.

Quinterno, J., & Orozco, V. (2012, April). *The great cost shift: How higher education cuts undermine the future middle class.* New York: Demos: An equal say and an equal chance for all.

Radford, A., Berkner, L., Wheeless, S., & Shepherd, B. (2010). *Persistence and attainment of 2003–04 beginning postsecondary students: After 6 years* (NCES 2011-151). Washington, DC: National Center for Educational Statistics. Retrieved from http://www.nces.ed.gov/pubs2011/2011151.pdf.

Ratcliff, J., Grace, J., Kehoe, J., Terenzini, P., & Associates. (1996). Realizing the potential: Improving postsecondary teaching, learning, and assessment. *Office of Educational Researcher and Improvement. The National Center on Post-Secondary Teaching, Learning, and Assessment.* Washington, DC: U.S. Government Printing Office.

Restad, P. (2014, July). "I don't like this one little bit." Tales from a flipped classroom. In Mary Bart (Ed.), *Faculty Focus special report: Blended and flipped: Exploring new models for effective teaching.* Magna Publication. http//www.FacultyFocus.com.

Rhem, J. (1995). Deep/surface approaches to learning: An introduction. *National Teaching and Learning Forum, 1*, 1–5.

Richardson, J. (2005, August). Instruments for obtaining student feedback: A review of the literature. *Assessment and Evaluation in Higher Education, 30*(4), 387–415.

Roach, R. (2014, January). Diverse analysis: Why President Obama's new community college plan matters. *The Chronicle of Higher Education.*

Robbins, S. B., Lauver, K., Le, H., Davis, D., Langley, R., & Carlstrom, A. (2004). Do psychosocial and study skill factors predict college outcomes? A meta-analysis. *Psychological Bulletin, 130*(2), 261–288.

Romainville, M. (2002, March/April). On the appropriate use of PISA. *Nouvelle Revue* (Brussels), 86–99.

Rouseff-Baker, F., & Holm, A. (2004, Summer). Engaging faculty and students in classroom assessment of learning. *New Directions for Community Colleges, 126*, 29–42.

Rovai, A. (2003, October). In search of higher persistence rates in distance education online programs. *The Internet and Higher Education, 6*(1).

Schudde, L., & Goldrick-Rab, S. (2017). Extending opportunity, perpetuating privilege: Institutional stratification amid educational expansion. In M. Bastedo, P. Altbach, P. Gumport, & B. Berdal (Eds.), *American Higher Education in the 21st Century.* Baltimore, MD: Johns Hopkins Press.

Scrivener, S., & Weiss, M., with Teres, J. (2009). *More guidance, better results? Three-year effects of an enhanced student services program at two community colleges.* New York: MDRC (Manpower Demonstration Research Corporation).

Secolsky, C., & Denison, B. (2011). *Handbook on measurement, assessment, and evaluation in higher education.* New York: Routledge.

Seidman, A. (Ed.). (2005). *College student retention: Formula for student success.* Westport, CT: American Council on Education, Praeger Publishing.

Seiler, V., & Seiler, M. (2002, Spring). Professors who make the grade. *Review of Business, 23*(2), 39.

Seybert, J. (2004, May/June). Has the time come for national benchmarking for community colleges? *Assessment Update, 15*(3), 12–14.

Shapiro, D., Dundar, A., Ziskin, M., Yuan, X., & Harrel A. (2013). *National Student Clearinghouse Research Center*—Signature Report #6, Completing College: A National View of Student Attainment Rates. https://www.nscresearchcenter.org/wp-content/uploads/NSC_Signature_Report_ 6.pdf.

Shea, P. (2015). A JOLT of new energy for the scholarship of online teaching and learning. Introduction. *Online Learning, 19*(3).

Shechter, O., Durik, A., Miyamoto, Y., & Harackiewicz, E. (2011). The role of utility value in achievement behavior: The importance of culture. *Personality and Social Psychology Bulletin, 37*(3), 303–317. https://www.pdfs.semanticscholar.org/.pdf.

Smith, S., &. Caruso. (2010). ECAR study of undergraduate students and information technology. EDUCAUSE, 6. Boulder, CO: Center for Applied Research. http://www.educause.edu/Resources/ECARStudyofUndergraduateStuden/217333.

Spooren, P., & Mortelmans, D. (2006, June). Will better students give higher ratings? *Educational Studies, 32*(2), 201–214.

Stiggins, R. (2005). *Student-involved assessment for learning* (4th ed.). Upper Saddle River, NJ: Pearson & Prentice Hall Publishers.

Street, J., Inthorn, S., & Scott, M. (2013). *From entertainment to citizenship: Politics and popular culture.* New York: Palgrave Macmillan.

Study Group on the Conditions of Excellence in American Higher Education. (1984). *Involvement in learning: Realizing the potential of American higher education. Final report of the Study Group on the Conditions of Excellence in American Higher Education.* Washington, DC: National Institute of Education.

Talbot, R. (2014, April/May). Toward a common definition of 'flipped learning' and flipped learning skepticism: Do students want to have lectures? A guide to the flipped classroom. *The Chronicle of Higher Education.*

Tan, K., & Prosser, M. (2004). Qualitatively different ways of differentiating student achievement: a phenomenologic study of academics' conceptions of grade descriptors. *Assessment & Higher Education, 29*(3).

Taylor, L., & Parsons, J. (2011). Improving student engagement. *Current Issues in Education, 14*(1). Retrieved from http://www.cie.asu.edu/.

Theall, M. (1999). New directions for theory and research on teaching: A review of the past twenty years. *New Directions for Teaching and Learning, 80*, 29–52.

Theall, M., & Centra, J. (2001). Assessing the scholarship of teaching: Valid decision from valid evidence. *New Directions for Teaching and Learning*, 86.

Thompson, R., & Serra, M. (2005, Summer). Use of course evaluations to assess the contributions of curricular and pedagogical initiatives to undergraduate general education learning objectives. *Education, 125*(4), 693.

Tinto, V. (1997, November/December). Classrooms as communities: Exploring the educational character of student persistence. *Journal of Higher Education, 68*(6), 599–623.

Tinto, V. (2000). Linking learning and leaving: Exploring the role of the college classroom in student departure. In Braxton (Ed.), *Reworking the student departure puzzle.* Nashville: Vanderbilt University Press.

Tinto, V. (2016, September). From retention to persistence. *Inside Higher Education.* https://www.insidehighered.com/views/2016/09/26/how-improve-student-persistence-and-com pletion-essay

Trochim, W. (2006, October). *The research methods knowledge base* (2nd ed.). http://www.social researchmethods.net/research/research.htm.

Tschannen-Moran, M., Hoy, A., & Hoy, N. (1998). Teacher efficacy: Its meaning and measure. *Review of Educational Research, 68*, 202–248.

United Nations Children's Fund (UNICEF). (2005). *Child poverty in rich countries 2005.* Florence, Italy: Innocenti Research Centre UNICEF.

Upcraft, M., Gardener, J., Barefoot, B., Cutright, M., & Morris, L. (2005). *Challenging and supporting the first year student.* San Francisco: Jossey-Bass.

U.S. Census Bureau. (2016). *Educational attainment and income and poverty in the United States.* http://www.census.gov/people.

Valcke, M. (2002). Cognitive load: Updating the theory? *Learning and Instruction.*

Van Middlesworth, C. (2003). Community college strategies: Assessing learning communities. *Assessment Update, 15*(2).

Volkwein, J. (2003, May). Implementing outcomes assessment on your campus. *The RP Group eJournal.* http://www.rpgroup/org/publications/ejournal/ Volume_1/volume_1.htm. (accessed 2006, March).

Walvoord, B. (2004). *Assessment clear and simple: A practical guide for institutions, departments, and general education.* San Francisco: Jossey-Bass.

Walvoord, B., & Johnson Anderson, V. (1998). *Effective grading: A tool for learning and assessment.* San Francisco: Jossey-Bass.

Weaver, D., Watts, W., & Maloney, P. (2001). In J. Shapiro, & J. Stefkovich (Eds.), *Ethical leadership and decision making in education: Applying theoretical perspectives to complex dilemmas,* 55–65. Mahwah, NJ: Lawrence Erlbaum.

Wieman, C. (2017). *Improving how universities teach science: Lessons from the Science Education Initiative.* Cambridge, MA: Harvard University Press.

Weimer, M. (2014, October). A few concerns about the rush to flip. Magna Pub., *Faculty Focus.*

Wendorf, C., & Alexander S. (2005). The influence of individual-and class-level fairness-related perceptions on student satisfaction. *Contemporary Educational Psychology, 30*(2), 190–206.

Wentzel, K., & Wigfield, A. (2009). *Handbook of motivation at school.* New York: Routledge.

Whiting. G. (1994). *Mastery learning: Thousands of students, thousands of excellent learners.* (Research report retrieved from ERIC, 07/19/06, ED425159).

Whitley, B. (2006). Principles of research in behavioral science (4th ed.). New York: McGraw-Hill, Inc.

Wiggins, G., & McTighe, J. (2007). *Schooling by design: Mission, action, and achievement.* Association for Supervision and Curriculum Development. Alexandria, VA: ASCD.

Wiggins, G. (2014). *Educative assessment: Designing assessments to inform and improve student performance.* San Francisco: Jossey-Bass.

Winne, P., & Nesbit, J. (2010). The psychology of academic achievement. *Annual Review of Psychology, 61,* 653–678.

Wulff, D., Jacobson, W., Freisem, K., Hatch, D., Lawrence, M., & Lenz, L. (Eds.). (2005). *Aligning for learning: Strategies for teaching effectiveness.* San Francisco: Jossey-Bass.

Xu, D., & Smith Jaggars, S. (2013, December). The impact of online learning on students' course outcomes: Evidence from a large community and technical college system. *Economics of Education Review, 37,* 46–57.

Young, M., & Zucker, S. (2004). *The standards-referenced interpretive framework: Using assessments for multiple purposes* (Harcourt Assessment Report). San Antonio, TX: Harcourt Assessment.

Yukselturk, E., Ozekes, S., & Turel, K. (2014, December). Predicting dropout student: An application of data mining methods in an online education program. *European Journal of Open, Distance and E-Learning, 17*(1).

Zimmerman, B., & Campillo, M. (2003). Motivating self-regulated problem solvers. In J. Davidson & R. Sternberg (Eds.), *The Nature of Problem Solving.* New York: Cambridge University Press.

Index

About the Author

Dr. S. deBoef earned graduate degrees in educational psychology and sociology and teaches psychology and sociology courses at a two-year college. She conducts research to develop strategies to enhance student learning outcomes because she believes that student success is critical for family and community well-being.